To

PAOLA'S REMEMBRANCES

By

Francesca Paolina Curatolo

From

Aunt Mary

© 2003 by Francesca Paolina Curatolo. All rights reserved.

No part of this book may be reproduced, stored in a retrieval system, or transmitted by any means, electronic, mechanical, photocopying, recording, or otherwise, without written permission from the author.

ISBN: 1-4107-0679-6 (E-book)
ISBN: 1-4107-0680-X (Paperback)

Library of Congress Control Number: 2002096819

This book is printed on acid free paper.

Printed in the United States of America
Bloomington, IN

1stBooks - rev. 03/17/03

Acknowledgments

I would like to thank my sisters Agatha Burks Leona Davison, my brother-in-law William Davison and nephew Charles Burks for their help in proof reading and editing of this book. I appreciate the support and encouragement of my sister Anna Popelka, and brothers Melchiore and Joseph Curatolo. I would like to express my appreciation to Anne Halligan, for taking the time to read the first draft of my manuscript and for her advice. To Francis Battisti a special thanks for your assistance and guidance.

Dedication

This book is dedicated:

To my loving mother
Paola Russo Curatolo

Thank you for the love, guidance and support you have given to our family and for the patience you have had with me during the writing of this book. Without your belief in me, this book would not have been written.

Authors Note

This book has taken shape over some five years. Writing this book sent me on a journey of discovery. It was on this journey that I came to an understanding of my mother.

I first decided to write about Mama while I was coming home from the hospital after one of her many stays. She had struggled with her illness, heart disease, for many years and I had come to realize that she might be leaving us soon.

When she came home from the hospital I asked her if she would tell me about her life in Sicily. She agreed and I started taping her voice. It was difficult for her as she was very weak. There were times when I did not understand what she was trying to tell me, so I repeatedly asked her the same thing over and over and she became frustrated with me. This experience of jogging her memories was quite a challenge for me, both good and bad.

This is a story of a young girl in Sicily who grew into a beautiful young woman. This young woman had the strength and courage to leave her family and her homeland and crossing the Atlantic Ocean at the age of 17, starting a new life in America. These are her Remembrances.

Francesca P. Curatolo

CHAPTER ONE

It was a warm and sunny January day. The sky was bright blue, with soft white clouds drifting by. I walked up the ship's gangway and looked up at the top of the ship where black smoke drifted out of the ship's funnels. They looked like giant chimneys. The size of the ship was overwhelming. I stepped on to the deck and made my way through the crowd of people who were bustling around me. My sister and I were immigrants going to a new country traveling steerage class and anxious to start our new life in America, but sad because we were leaving our family. I glanced over to my sister Agata who was walking beside me.

"Agata, I'm so excited we are going to America," I said.

"I'm excited too," said Agata.

We made our way to the front of the ship's railing where the passengers were standing throwing brightly colored confetti streamers. My sister and I had never been on our own and I felt as if I was in a dream. We were filled with excitement, happy and frightened at the same time. We looked down at the sea and saw a small boat coming toward the ship. As it drew closer, we could see there was only one passenger in the middle of the boat. The boat stopped and a woman stood up. To our surprise it was our mother, who had hired a boat to take her out to the ship to see her daughters before they left on their journey. Ma searched the faces standing at the railing and finally she saw us. She waved at us and started to cry. . . tears ran down her cheeks. I saw the pain on her face and my heart felt as if it was going to break. My hands gripped the ship's railing and I stood frozen . . . I couldn't move, tears filled my eyes. Agata turned to me and she was crying too. This was the last time we saw our mother.

My thoughts turned to the home I had left and I could picture the street where we lived, Via Mannina. The houses on the narrow cobblestone street stood side by side. Some of the houses had balconies. I looked through the front door of my house and saw a large table in the center of the room. Ma and Pa were sitting at a corner of the table eating out of one large dish. It was the custom for husband and wives to eat out of the same plate. My brother Camillo and sisters Rosina, Francesca and Annina were sitting at the table. Ma made sure that each child had their plates filled with equal portions of food.

I remembered the aroma of freshly baked bread coming from the stone oven that was in the wall and filling the room. Next to the oven was an iron framework that supported a grill. A pot of pasta was cooking over the wood burning flame. Along side the grill was a small braciera, or barbecue that had fish stew and sauce simmering. There was an archway on one side of the room that had a curtain drawn across it. This was my mother and father's bedroom. Agata's and my bedroom was next to Ma and Pa's room. In our bedroom there was a large bed and my mother's steamer trunk. Rosina and Francesca were babies, and when they grew up they moved into our room.

One day Pa decided to make the upstairs storage room into a bedroom. Our bedroom had become too small for all of us and there were times that I had to sleep on top of Ma's trunk. We ran upstairs and began to arrange the furniture, two beds and a dresser that Pa bought us. I drew some pictures and put them on the walls and Rosina put some flowers she picked on the dresser. Rosina, Francesca and I spent many happy times in this room playing and talking. There was a small window that faced the Gulf of Castellammare and when I looked out the window I could see a tranquil and calm sea, but there were times the sea raged — waves breaking and crashing on to the shore. We called those waves, *cavallo di mare*, sea horses. Agata remained in the bedroom downstairs while Annina, the baby slept in Ma and Pa's room.

Under the steps that led upstairs to my room was an arch. Behind the arch was a room with a small bed where my brother Camillo slept.

The *cesso* (the toilet) was in a corner of the house. We did not have running water. I remember going to the public water faucet in the village, which was a mile and a half from our home and carrying a jug of water to my home. It was very heavy and I had to stop to rest it on the sharp stones on the road which penetrated the jug. By the time I reached home the jug was half empty and I was soaking wet. That is when my mother decided to buy us a wooden jug.

Along the coast overlooking the sea was a castle with cannons on top of it. In ancient times the Saracens, who were very tall people, lived in the castle. My mother told me when there was a Queen in Sicily she lived in this castle. Steps led down from the castle to a cove that had a stone wall surrounding it and this is where the Queen would bathe. They called the cove *La Vasca Della Regina* (the Queen's Pool). No one lived in the castle when I was young so we would walk down the steps to the *Vasca Della Regina* and bathe in the calm waters of the sea.

Further along the beach were steps leading to the *Banchina* (the wharf) where the big ships anchored in the gulf had their mooring ropes tied to a large iron wheel. Around the other side of the cove on the beach were the *magazzinos* (small warehouses) where the fishermen stored their fishing nets and other equipment. I remember walking with my mother and sisters on this beach where we saw the fishermen mending their nets. At the end of the warehouses were more steps. They led to the street where there was a church, the 'Annunziata'. Beyond the church the street separated, one road led to the houses in the village and the other down to the beach. From the beach you could see the small fishing boats anchored in the sea. Further down the beach was another private cove surrounded by large stones, where we went to bathe. Ma sat on the beach and kept a watchful eye on us as we didn't know how to swim.

Next to this cove was a flat stretch of grass where the fishermen threw the fishing nets to dry.

The hills and mountains in Castellammare were covered with various kinds of trees and bushes, like Manna trees and Juniper shrubs. On the edge of the mountain cliff was a lighthouse that faced the sea. Olive groves and grape vineyards were on the level ground in the *campagna* (the country) along with orange, lemon, grapefruit trees, black mulberry trees, fig trees and prickly pear on cacti. I loved living in Castellammare Del Golfo with its clear blue waters, white sandy beaches and large rocks and cliffs. Castellammare is a splendor of nature where the mountains touch the sea. From March to October little rain falls and the air is dry because of a hot dry wind called the *Sirocco,* that blows across the Mediterranean Sea from the deserts of North Africa. When the warm tropical breeze flowed across Castellammare, it felt wonderful, like a loving caress on your cheek. You would want to stay in this tropical paradise forever.

Francesca Paolina Curatolo

**Castellammare del Golfo
Sicily**

CHAPTER TWO

Our house was not far from the seashore, we could hear the fishermen sing their chants as they pulled their fishing boats onto the shore.

My father made his living as a fishmonger (a fish peddler.) Pa went down to the Marina to see what fish he was going to get that day. He had two large baskets, which he used for the fish he was going to sell that day.

"Mateo, Gaspere, what kind of fish do you have for me today?" asked Pa.

"Sardines and Whiting," said Matteo.

"I have Mackerel and Calamari," said Gaspere.

"I'll take some Mackerel and Whiting," Pa said.

He filled the baskets with the fish and carried them to our house where he prepared himself for the long journey to the village of Alcamo. When he came into the kitchen I was waiting for him.

"Pa, let me help you," I said.

"Let me put the baskets down," said Pa.

I was ready with a cord similar to a clothesline and I gave it to him. He tied the baskets together. Then he put sacks over the top of each basket securing them so the fish wouldn't spill out. He placed a sack filled with dried seaweed, which he had made to protect his shoulders over his head, then he put the baskets on his shoulders. I can still see him with the baskets on his shoulders running bare foot up the road to Alcamo. He didn't wear shoes because without them he could run faster.

When Pa reached Alcamo he stopped to put his shoes on. He made his way down the crowded cobblestone street where he set up his stand. His customers respected him, as they knew the fish he sold them were always fresh.

It was approaching late afternoon and most of the street vendors had sold all their goods and they were closing their stands. Papa had sold the last fish and gathering the empty baskets, he put them on his shoulders and started walking home. Along the side of the road were some grapes and black raspberries. He stopped to cut some and put them in the empty baskets. Sometimes he'd stop at a tavern to rest and eat, but most of the time he came straight home.

It was dusk and we were anxious for my father to return home. We wanted to hear all about what he saw while he was there. I was outside the house and saw him coming up the road.

"Agata, Rosina, Francesca! hurry, Pa is coming!"

We all ran to meet him.

"Pa, let us help you with the baskets," I said.

My father was happy to see us and smiled as he put the baskets down. Tired after his long trip, but happy to be home, he sat in his chair. I saw that his feet and legs were dirty and bruised from the stones on the dirt road. I ran quickly to get a basin of water to wash his feet and legs. I bathed his feet and applied ointment to his bruises. Pa was resting in his chair and we gathered around him.

PAOLA'S REMEMBRANCES

"Tell us what you saw in Alcamo. What news did you hear?" asked Agata.

Pa smiled as he leaned back in his chair. He started to tell us what he had heard, but Ma called to us.

"Supper is ready. Come and eat," said Ma.

We sat down at the table bowed our heads and made the sign of the cross. Rosina and Francesca were talking while we were eating when Ma interrupted them.

"You should not talk while you are eating, otherwise you will miss a mouthful of food," said Ma.

Mama was cleverly telling us that it was not polite to talk with our mouths full of food. Rosina and Francesca said they were sorry, but they wanted to hear about Papa's trip. Papa told us after supper he was going down to the Marina to see Don Peppino Vasille and when he returned he would tell us about his trip.

Supper was over and we helped Ma put the leftover food away. Pa left the house and walked down to Don Vasille's office, where all the fishmongers brought the money that they had made selling the fish. He'd count the money and take his share of the money and give Pa his. Don Vasille was a very rich person who had property and was a man of means. When there was a holiday Don Vasille would give Papa a bottle of homemade wine.

Don Vasille said, "Melchiore, bring an empty bottle with you next time you are down at the Marina and I will give you some wine to take home."

"Si, Don Peppino tomorrow I will bring the bottle... *Baciamo le Mani*,"

(I kiss your hands) said Pa.

They shook hands and Pa left Don Peppino and came home. When we'd say, *Baciamo le Mani*, it was showing respect to the person. This was said only to the rich and the elderly.

Papa came home with his half of the money he had worked so hard for and gave it to my mother. Ma took care of all the household needs. She bought our food such as wheat, fava beans, figs, carob and olive oil. The next day my father went to see Don Peppino Vasille and brought him the empty wine bottle.

"*Buon Giorno*, I see you brought your wine bottle," said Don Peppino. He filled the bottle with wine and gave it to my father.

"*Tanti Grazie*, (many thanks)," said Pa.

Pa left and went to the *magazzino* where he met my brother Camillo. It was March and the sardines were in season. A sardine company hired Pa and Camillo to salt sardines and put them into large wooden barrels. The company then shipped them out to their customers around Sicily and the world. When Pa and Camillo finished working the company gave them a sack of sardines to take home.

My father brought home many kinds of fish. Here are a few recipes Mama made. They are simple and the oil she used was olive oil.

WHITING— — MERLUZZO -Fish Soup

1 clove garlic ¼ Cup fresh parsley 2 Tbs. oil
salt & pepper to taste one 2 lb. fish 2 qt. water

Clean fish remove the insides rinse and cut into 2 to 3 pieces including the head. Place oil, garlic, and parsley in a pan and sauté until soft. Add water to the pan and bring to a boil, add salt, pepper and fish. Cook for about 15 minutes.

MACKEREL — SGOMBRO

One 2 lb. mackerel 4 Fresh cut up tomatoes
  salt, pepper, oregano, oil
2 cloves garlic 1 small onion sliced

In a sauce pan that has a little oil add tomatoes, salt, pepper, oregano, garlic and onion. Cook for 10 to 15 minutes. Cut the clean fish into 2 to 3 pieces and place fish in the saucepan along with the above ingredients. Cook for 15 minutes.

FRESH ROASTED SARDINES — SARDI ARROSTITE

Place clean sardines on a wire rack. Season with salt, pepper and olive oil. Roast over a hot flame on the grill. Serve with hot homemade Italian bread.

Francesca Paolina Curatolo

SARDINE — SARDI a la GHIOTTA

To prepare fresh sardines for cooking cut the fins, remove the scales and bones, slit the belly and remove the innards, rinse and season with salt and pepper.

1 onion chopped   ¼ cup olive oil
1 cup plain tomato sauce
Salt and black pepper 6 Sardines   4 cup water

In a medium pot sauté onion in olive oil until golden brown. Add tomato sauce and a little water. Cook 5 to10 minutes. Add the cleaned sardine pieces to the sauce. Season with salt and pepper to taste. Cook for an additional 10 minutes.

PAOLA'S REMEMBRANCES

**The Banchina (wharf)
Castellammare del Golfo
Sicily**

CHAPTER THREE

One terrible day my father was bitten by a rabid dog. Mama had to take him to Palermo, as there were no doctors or hospitals in Castellammare. I don't recall who stayed with us while they were gone. It may have been my older half sister Brigita, or Vincenza. When my mother and father returned home they brought us presents. I was so happy to see them. Ma gave me a little doll the size of a Barbie doll. I made little dresses for my doll out of scraps of material and I hand sewed them together.

I was six years old when I started going to school. I did well in my studies, and my mother wanted me to become a teacher, but I did not want to. I stopped going to school after the third grade, which is like the fifth grade in America.

I remember one time it was raining and we were going to school. Papa was standing in the house and he was wearing a large dark blue cape with a hood attached to it. He looked so tall and handsome.

"I will take you to school," said Pa.

We all got under his cape which he wrapped around us to keep us dry. He did many thoughtful things for us.

I loved my brother and sisters very much. We had many happy times together. My sister Francesca was very pretty and we called her, *Pupa del la catalogo*, which means catalog doll. My sister Annina was called *Chiacchierone* (chatterbox) she never stopped talking. They called me *La Mansueta*, the meek quiet one. I thought before I spoke and when I had something to say, I said it.

When I was nine years old my mother decided to send me to a dressmaker, where I learned the art of dressmaking. Everyday, except Saturday and Sunday, I'd go to the dressmaker's, Signorina Francesca's house. The first thing I learned was how to press dress pleats and to cut out dress patterns. Signorina Francesca was a very devout Christian, a kind and patient woman. After our lesson she would take us to church.

I was a faithful church follower and joined the Daughters of Mary Society. The Society gave me a religious booklet called, *The Sacred Story* and a medal that had *Children of Mary* inscribed on it. A ribbon hung from the medal and I wore it around my neck.

Our house was on the street behind Signorina Francesca's house. I could see my house from her window. Many times I'd hear my mother calling me, Paolina. She wanted me to come home to make bread. I was nine years old and I enjoyed making bread. The girls in my class couldn't believe that I could make bread, because I was so young. They said to me, "You make bread? But you are too young."

"Paolina, your mother is calling you. You may leave, go see what she needs," said Signorina Francesca.

"*Grazie*," I said.

I left Signorina Francesca's house and went home where Mama was waiting for me.

Francesca Paolina Curatolo

I put my apron on and went to the cupboard where we kept the flour. I brought the flour over to the wooden pastry board that Mama had set up for me between two chairs as the table was too high for me. I poured twenty five pounds of flour into a big sifter, a little at a time and sifted the flour onto the pastry board. For the 25 pounds of flour, I used a pound of starter yeast that was given to us by a woman my mother knew. The lady asked us to replace the yeast, or if she didn't need the yeast, we would give her a loaf of freshly made bread.

One day I was making bread and I was having a difficult time handling the dough, as my hands were small. Mama saw this and called to my sister Agata who was sitting in her room embroidering to come and help me.

"Agata, help your sister," said Ma.

We called Agata, *Salto Diviato*, it means to jump quickly, it was her nature to quickly snap back.

"No! I have to finish my embroidering," said Agata.

"It's all right Ma. I can do it myself," I said.

Making bread with my mother is one of my fondest memories. I remember her gathering grape branches tying them into bundles and putting them in the storage room upstairs. When we made bread we'd use the grape branches as fuel in the stone oven. Mama taught me how to shape the dough into braids, round loaves, small buns and little baskets. After the bread had risen, we put it into the hot stone oven and attached an iron door to the front of the oven. The smell of the bread was wonderful. Ma took a loaf of freshly baked bread out of the oven sliced it and drizzled olive oil over it. I couldn't wait to taste the delicious bread.

When I was older I made homemade pasta every night, but one night when I went to the cupboard to get the flour I found there wasn't enough.

"Ma, there isn't enough flour to make the pasta," I said.

"All right, go to the store and buy some pasta and tomorrow I will go to the storehouse to buy wheat," said Ma.

The next morning Ma got up early; Pa had gone down to the Marina.

"I am going to the storehouse to buy some wheat and I will be back soon. Clean up the breakfast dishes and be ready to go with me to the mill when I return," said Ma.

The wheat had to be taken to the mill where it was ground into flour. We had just finished straightening the room when Ma came in the door. She had a big sack of wheat in her arms. The sack was too heavy for one person to carry to the mill, which was about three miles away, so she divided the wheat into smaller sacks.

"Rosina, Paolina, it's time to go to the mill," said Ma.

It was a quiet and peaceful morning. Not very many people were on the road. The birds were singing and the air was warm. As we walked along the road we saw a little shrine, a *Cappella*. It had a picture of *Santa Nicola* in the shrine.

"I'm tired, let's stop and rest," I said.

Francesca Paolina Curatolo

We stopped to rest on the side of the road, and as I sat down on the road, I looked around and saw how beautiful the country was. There were fields of grass and wild flowers all around us.

"Let's go, the mill is not very far, we'll be there in no time," said Ma.

Finally we reached the mill where there was a large grinding machine. Ma took the sacks of wheat from us and climbed the stairs that led to the top of the grinding machine and poured the wheat into the top of the grinder.

"Paolina, Rosina be ready with the flour sacks to catch the wheat," said Ma.

"We're ready," I said.

The ground wheat started down the chute and went into the sacks we were holding. Ma divided the flour so we could carry it and she took the heaviest of the sacks for herself.

Next to the mill was a beautiful vineyard that had a six foot wall around it. Gorgeous pink roses were growing up and over the top of the wall and luscious white grapes were hanging from the grapevines.

"Paolina, let's pick some of the flowers," said Rosina.

I laughed. "They are too high, I can't reach them."

We made this trip to the mill many times. Occasionally we would get a ride on a Sicilian *carretto* (cart), but most of the time we would walk. The Sicilian *carrettos* were decorated with bright colors, red, yellow and blue plumes, bells and gaily colored ribbons. The panels were adorned with paintings of Saints and bearded knights on them. Feather tufted mules drew the carts.

Upon our return home Mama separated the flour into three groups. The first was the fine flour we used in making bread and pasta. The second was coarser used for *muffolette*, a heavier type of bread. The third was the coarsest and used to feed the chickens.

We had a rooster and some chickens outside our house in a cage. The hen had stopped laying and my mother knew it was time for the chicks to hatch. Ma brought the hen into the house and made a nest of straw in a basket and put the hen on the eggs. The chicken wouldn't eat while on her eggs, so Ma force fed her fava beans. It was time for the chicks to hatch and I called my sisters.

"Francesca, Rosina, Agata, look! The chicks are pecking their shells."

They all ran to see the chicks. We were happy to see them hatch because we wanted to hold them. They were cute and fuzzy.

My mother was a talented and resourceful person. She'd cut out material and she'd hand sew the material making clothes for her children. One day she went to the fabric shop to purchase some material. She wanted to make a suit for my brother Camillo. Now making a suit was not easy and she knew she needed some help. My mother's cousin Paola, who was a tailor, lived about a mile from us. It was in the afternoon around 2:00 o'clock and Mama went over to her house. She knocked on the door and Paola came to the door.

"Buon Giorno," how are you? I have brought some material to make a suit for my son and I need some help. Will you please cut it out for me?" asked Ma.

"Yes, it will be my pleasure," said Paola. "Come on in and sit down."

Ma sat down at the kitchen table and gave Paola the material. She laid the material out and started cutting out the suit. Ma asked how her family was and Paola told her everyone was well. Paola finished cutting the material and gave it to my mother.

"Grazie," said Ma.

Mama got up from the table put the material in a bag and thanked Paola again. She started to leave and was half way out the door when Paola stopped her.

"Wait a minute, I have some dried figs for you to take home," said Paola.

"Thank you again, *buona sera* (good night)," said Ma.

It was dusk and the sun had set. Ma started walking down the street when she saw my sisters and me coming to meet her. We ran to her and hugged her. She was happy to see us. It was a beautiful balmy evening and we held hands as we walked talking and laughing all the way to our house. Papa and Camillo were sitting at the kitchen table waiting for us. We had supper ready, as we knew Ma would be coming home late. After supper we went outside to enjoy the beautiful night. The moon was out and the stars were twinkling brightly in the sky. They seemed so close one could just reach up and touch them. It was getting late and Ma told us to come in the house. We went in and kissed our parents goodnight and went to bed.

I woke up to the sound of birds singing. I hurriedly put my dress and shoes on and went downstairs. My mother was busy sewing Camillo's suit. When she finished making the suit, Camillo put it on. It was a perfect fit and he looked handsome in it. Camillo changed and went down to the Marina, where Pa was waiting for him.

"Paolina, *caffé* (coffee) is ready and the bread is on the table," said Ma.

Outside the house I heard sheep bleating.

"Ma, do you want me to go and buy some milk?" I asked.

"Yes, here is some money," said Ma.

I went outside and there were sheep in front of our house. The owner was herding them down the street toward the hills. "*Signore*, I would like to buy some milk," I said.

"Give me your container and I will fill it for you," he said.

I gave him the jar and he milked the sheep while I waited. "Thank you, *Signore*."

I paid him and took the milk into the house.

My sisters had come downstairs and they were sitting at the table eating their breakfast.

"Where is Camillo?" Rosina asked.

"He is down at the Marina with your father," replied Ma.

"Sit down and have your breakfast, Paolina," said Ma.

Francesca Paolina Curatolo

I sat down at the table and ate my breakfast. When we finished eating breakfast my sisters and I cleared the table.

I went upstairs to my room to get my crochet and came back downstairs to the kitchen where Ma was waiting for me. I sat down and started to crochet when I noticed that I had made a mistake in the row I was crocheting.

"Ma, will you help me? I am having a little trouble with this row," I said.

"Si, but I need to send you to the store to buy cotton crochet thread. Today I am going to show you how to crochet stockings," Ma said.

My mother had bought wool from one of the sheep owners. She had washed the wool and put it outside to dry on the grass. Some of the wool was used for filling mattresses and pillows. She had gathered the rest and spun it into yarn. She used a bamboo stick that had a slit in the top of it. The wool was put on the top of the stick and with her hands she pulled the wool, stretching twisting and turning it. She gathered it onto a hand held spindle that had a hook at one end and a wheel on the other. She removed the wool from the spindle and wrapped it around a small *teldio* (a loom). The skein of wool was then moistened with water and when the wool dried she gathered it into a ball. Holding the hand spindle against the side of her thigh she twisted the wool and cotton thread together gathering it onto the spindle.

Agata and I left the house and went to the store and on the way we met my friend Fifidria.

"Fifidria, will you be home this afternoon?" I asked.

"Si, come over when you can," said Fifidria.

Agata and I returned home with the crochet thread and spent the rest of the morning crocheting and sewing.

That afternoon I asked Ma if we could go over to my friend Fifidria's house. Fifidria and I were the same age and very good friends. She said yes and Rosina and I walked down the street to her house.

"Fifidria, Fifidria," I called.

Fifidria came to the door. "Hello," said Fifidria. "I will be right out."

We walked down to the Villa that was at the end of our street. It was three blocks wide and so long that it went all the way to *Corso Garibaldi* street. An iron gate was in front of the Villa attached to a very high wall that surrounded it. The gate opened to reveal a garden filled with beautiful flowers. A small caretaker's house was in the garden. One of the trees was next to the wall where we were playing. Small white blossoms were on the tree. They had a hole in the center of the blossoms and they had fallen outside the wall onto the ground. We picked up the blossoms and put them into our aprons as we were going to make flower necklaces, when I heard my mother calling us.

"We have to go home we will see you tomorrow Fifi," I said.

Fifidria did not play with us anymore that summer because she had a heart condition and died at the age of twelve. When Fifidria died I could not bring myself to go and see her. . I was afraid. The funeral procession was coming down the street and when I heard the music the band was playing, I started to cry and couldn't stop. I had lost my best friend.

Anna and Melchiore Russo

CHAPTER FOUR

It was a warm Saturday afternoon and we were outside playing when Mama called to us.

"The horse races are going to start in an hour, do you want to go?" Ma said.

"Si," we yelled.

Mama, my sisters and I walked down to the main street *Corso Garibaldi*, where the horse races took place. Along the sides of the road were wooden barriers protecting the people watching the race. The owners who were aristocrats, were preparing their horses. The horses dressed in their finery raced without riders on them and occasionally one would go wild and jump over the barrier into the crowd of people. I was excited but a little afraid the horses would jump the barrier in front of us and that we would get hurt, so I stood near my mother to watch. Between races we sat on the chairs we had brought with us. My mother gave us money to buy some roasted chickpeas, or roasted pumpkin seeds. I liked the *torrone*, the sweet honey almond nougat candy.

It was twilight when the races were over and we were going home. I wish that Pa could have been with us. We had such a good time, but he had to work.

When we walked in the front door Pa was sitting at the kitchen table waiting for us. Ma told us to get ready for bed because tomorrow was Sunday and we were going to early Mass.

The sun shone through the window and woke me up. I hurried and got ready for church. I went down to the kitchen where the smell of *caffé* greeted me. I quickly drank the *caffé* and went out the door.

Mass was over and we came home from church. Agata helped Francesca and Annina change from their Sunday clothes. Agata, being the eldest daughter, had certain responsibilities. She helped my mother cook and take care of the younger children. Rosina and I were old enough to take care of ourselves.

"Ma, may I go visit *Zia*, (Aunt) Ninfa?" asked Rosina.

Zia Ninfa Scolaro, my mother's sister lived about two miles from our house. In front of her house was a grape arbor with big bunches of beautiful white grapes.

"Si, but Paolina must go with you," said Ma.

Rosina and I walked arm in arm down the road toward my aunt's house.

We were very close. She was two years younger than me and we went many places together. Rosina was taller than all of us and we had a nickname for her, *Schrovio*, it means having long legs. Finally we arrived at *Zia's* house.

"Come in, come in," said *Zia*.

My mother had given us some fish to take to her sister.

"*Zia*, Ma sent you these fish," I said.

"*Grazie*, come in," said *Zia*.

We went in the house and joined my cousins who were sitting around the table. *Zia* gave us some fruit and a glass of water.

"Let's go outside. It's such a beautiful day," said Cousin Angelina.

"*Con permisso*, (with your permission) please excuse us *Zia* Ninfa," I said.

We went outside and played with our cousins. It was getting dark and it was time for us to go home.

"We have to go *Zia*," I said.

"I have grapes and figs I want to give you before you leave," said Zia.

I kissed my aunt.

"*Ossa mi Benedica*," I said.

"*Dio ti Benedica*," she said.

We were taught to respect our elders and this was a way to show respect to them. *Ossa mi Benedica*, means bless me and the response *Dio ti Benedica* is God blesses you. We said good-bye to our cousins and went home. We had a lovely afternoon with them.

It was August 21st. . . . we sang as *La processione dell Addolorata*, the procession of the Addolorata went by on this Holy day. The roses opened and the petals fell and Mary ascended into heaven, and when Mary was with her friends she embraced them and blessed them.

Four strong men walked by us holding poles on their shoulders that had a platform on them with the statue of Mary holding the crucified Jesus. Men and women who made a promise to the Virgin Mary and Jesus carried lighted candles, large and small, depending on what they had promised. The

PAOLA'S REMEMBRANCES

crowds of people shouted "Viva, Hosanna," as they passed by. When the procession was over we went home. Many of our religious holidays were celebrated with processions. They were part of our culture and it was a time of joy for us.

September had suddenly come upon us and was the month the grapes were harvested. Each year Camillo and I would go to the vineyard and pick the grapes.

It was early in the morning the sun had not risen. I awoke to my mother's voice calling me. Camillo and I were going to the grape vineyard for the harvesting of grapes.

"Paolina, get up! Your brother is waiting for you," said Ma.

I got dressed and went downstairs where Camillo was waiting for me in the kitchen. We started off down the road. It took about an hour for us to walk to the *campagna* (country), where the grapes were. The sun was rising when we arrived at the vineyard. I had a special knife I brought with me to cut the grapes. Camillo didn't cut the grapes. His job was to crush them by stomping them with special shoes he would wear. The shoes had nails on the bottom of the shoes. Camillo was paid more money for doing this than I was for picking the grapes.

The owner of the vineyard had donkeys and one of the laborers brought a donkey to where I was picking the grapes. Large baskets were strapped to the donkey's sides. The grapes I had picked were in a big basket on the ground. I emptied the grapes from the basket into the ones on the donkey.

It was lunch time and everyone stopped to eat. We walked to the warehouse where in the large room they served us our meals. It took two or three days to pick the grapes, so we spent the nights sleeping on the hard floor in this room. They didn't give us any bedding, but it was warm, so we didn't need a blanket. The owner slept in a separate room on a bed.

In a corner of the room was a large vat filled with grapes. The vat had a drain in it where the juice came out into a receptacle. Camillo was one of many who climbed into the vat and crushed the grapes.

One time my brother Camillo and I were working in another vineyard and the owners gave us a small loaf of bread for us to eat in the morning. I ate a little and saved the rest of the bread for the remainder of the day. That evening after a long tiring day of picking grapes we went to the warehouse where they gave us a dish of pasta to eat. The harvesting was done and the owners gave us grapes to take home. Our family was happy to see us and we were glad to be home. When my mother saw me she was concerned because I lost weight. Mama took the grapes from us and we sat down to have something to eat. She hung some of the grapes on a rope across the room upstairs. When the grapes became dry, and became raisins, she would let us eat them.

The next day my brother went to the owner of the vineyard to collect our wages. The owner gave him more money then was due us. He explained that I had eaten less than the other workers and I deserved the extra money. I thought the loaf of bread was supposed to last me all day!

Around the middle of October, Camillo, Rosina, my father and I went to the campagna to pick olives. The olives were black and green, ready for picking. It was very early in the morning and the sun had just risen. Rosina and I walked up the road with our arms around each other holding each other up, trying to stay awake. Pa and Camillo laughed at us as we stumbled up the road. The olive grove was a long distance from where we lived and would have to spend the night.

We arrived at the olive grove and started working right away. Pa and Camillo climbed the ladders that were against the trees and pulled the olives off the branches letting them fall to the ground. Rosina and I were on our hands and knees gathering them and putting them into our baskets. When our baskets were full we took them to the farmhouse. Rosina and I had a lot of fun working in the olive grove. We were happy that we were able to help our family make some money.

One time we were picking olives at another olive grove, my father was on the ladder reaching for the olives when the branch broke and he fell to the ground scraping his arms. Rosina and I thought it was funny and started laughing. Camillo was picking olives in the same tree as my father and when he saw Pa falling he started to laugh, too. I know we shouldn't have laughed. Pa could have hurt himself badly.

"Paolina, Rosina, go to the farm house and tell Mr. Palermo I fell out of the tree," said Pa.

Francesca Paolina Curatolo

We quickly ran to the farmhouse.

"Mr. Palermo, Mr. Palermo, come quick! My father fell out of the tree," I said.

The owners of the olive grove, Mr. & Mrs. Palermo were frightened and they hurried down to the grove where my father was. They were old but came as quickly as they could. Mr. Palermo brought a lantern filled with oil and Mrs. Palermo had bandages. They used the oil from the lantern on my father's arms and wrapped them with the bandages. Camillo, Rosina, and I continued working as Pa rested before he climbed back on the ladder. When we finished picking the olives, Mr. & Mrs. Palermo paid my father.

Pa told us to get ready as we were going home. We started to leave the olive grove when Mr. Palermo stopped us. He gave my father some olives to take home.

Finally we arrived home tired, but happy to see Mama and our sisters. Rosina and I went up to our room to rest while Mama prepared supper. Papa gave Mama the olives we brought home from the olive grove and after we finished eating she started the process of curing the olives. She put the olives into an earthen jar, with salt, garlic, and oil. We had to wait until they were cured before we could eat them.

It was my birthday on November 9th and my godfather; Joseph Curatolo (no relation to my husband) came to our home. He brought me a little doll made out of Manna for my birthday. I was thrilled getting such a nice present.

PAOLA'S REMEMBRANCES

"Ma, did *Padrino*, (Godfather) make the doll?" I asked.

"No, he bought in a store," said Ma.

Ma explained that the doll was made from manna juice and the juice came from the Manna Ash trees that grow on the hillsides. In the summer they put a hook in the back of the tree and the sweetish manna juice comes out of the tree. When the juice sets it turns into a solid form. If it starts to rain the Manna has to be gathered quickly because it melts.

That evening after we had finished eating supper, my mother told us stories. It was dark outside and she lit the kerosene filled *lume* (lamp) and set it on top of the table. Ma could not read because she did not go to school, but she told us the stories handed down through the generations of her family. We sat around the kitchen table and listened intently to her stories. I remember her telling us fairy tales, Rapunzel, Cinderella and Hansel and Gretel. She also told us Bible stories about Jesus. It was time for us to go to bed, we were happy and tired after a long day.

I awoke to the sound of rain beating on the roof of the house. I looked out the window and saw the seas fierce waves pounding the shore. I saw fishing boats sinking in the sea and the fishermen being tossed around like toys. They were struggling in the storm tossed sea, fighting their way toward the shore. I got dressed and went downstairs where Ma and Pa told us that everything was being done to save the seamen. The storm lasted all day and into the night.

The next day when I woke up the sun was shining brightly and things had settled down after the terrible storm. The fishermen were back on their boats and had gone out to the sea to fish.

December was here and we were looking forward to the upcoming holidays. Mama had saved some extra money and she went to the store to buy food that we did not have during the year, such as meat that she cooked in sauce. We were excited, looking forward to celebrating the holidays. The first holiday was December 13th, the Holy Day of Santa Lucia. Ma prepared chickpeas, fava beans and cuccia, Saint Lucy's pudding with *vino cotto.* On Santa Lucia's day only these foods were eaten.

Two more weeks and Christmas would be upon us. Mama was busy making Christmas fig cookies that she shaped into birds, dolls and baskets. She cut them and pinched the ends and decorated them with colored sugar sprinkles. On Christmas day we went to church. When we came home we sat down to eat the special Christmas dinner Ma had prepared for us. She gave each one of us a Christmas fig cookie that she had made. We didn't exchange gifts like we do in America, but this was a special day for all of us. *Nona*, Grandmother Paola, my mother's mother came to visit us. She was old and I do not remember very much about her, but I do remember that she was very short. She gave us dry salted chickpeas she had in her dress pocket.

Easter was another important holiday too. Ma made Easter breadbaskets that had a colored hard boiled egg in the center and little lambs made out of bread dough. Ma made our little house into a home full of love.

Nona Paola's sister lived in the mountains, her name was Rosa, and we went to visit *Zia* Rosa. It took us about half an hour to walk to her home. Ma gave us some fish to give her aunt and cousins and they were happy to see us. The house looked just like Heidi's grandfather's house in the movie of Heidi.

There were times my mother would send Rosina and me alone to *Zia's* house. She could see *Zia's* house on the mountainside from our house and she watched to see that Rosina and I arrived safely.

One day Papa asked me to write to his children who had left Sicily, and ask them to send some money to him. He was getting old and needed help. It was hard for him to work and he was angry because they did not help him. He told me to write to them and say, "One father fed thirteen children and thirteen children do not know how to feed one father." Occasionally Girolamo and Brigita would send him money and the rest of the children would write to him.

Girolamo my half brother lived in Detroit, Michigan. Girolamo wrote and told us he had sent us a package addressed to his wife's relatives and asked how we liked what he sent. Ma went to the Girolamo's relatives and asked them for the package. They told her that they didn't have it. Finally they admitted they had received the package and had opened it and they decided to keep what was in the package.

"Do you have any of the material left?" Ma asked.

They said yes and gave her what was left.

Ma wanted to make a skirt from the material for my sister Agata. She asked my father's niece Marietta, if she would cut a skirt out of the material. Marietta agreed and she came to our house, laid the silky white material on the kitchen floor and cut out a bell shaped skirt. Ma hand sewed the skirt and when she was finished Agata happily put the skirt on. I can see her twirling around and around.

Our family was not rich in material things, but the love we shared for one another made us a rich family. My father was an honest man, loving father and good husband. He worked hard to provide for us and never took charity.

My mother was an attractive woman tall and stately. She wore her dark brown hair pulled back and tied in a bun at the nape of her neck. Her eyes were brown. Ma was kind and generous a loving wife and mother. Her family and friends had much respect for her.

CHAPTER FIVE

Camillo was eighteen years old when he joined the Italian Army. Mama decided she would pay him a visit in Catania, where he was stationed. She asked me to write a letter to him, telling him when she would be arriving. We went to the train station and watched her board the train. She was carrying a large sack filled with homemade bread sticks for Camillo and his friends.

Camillo was waiting for Mama at the train station. The station was crowded and people were hurriedly getting off the train. Mama started walking down the train steps with the heavy sack and almost fell. Camillo ran to her quickly and took the sack from her. She was happy to see him and she kissed and embraced him. Camillo took her into town where they spent a few hours together, and then Mama returned home.

Camillo was in the army for only a few months when he became ill. The doctors examined him and they found that he was anemic. They decided to give him a leave and sent him home.

Camillo left Catania and took the train home. We didn't know he was coming and when he came into the house we were surprised and shocked. He looked terrible; his face was pale and gaunt.

Ma started giving orders to us. "We are going to do all we can to help your brother regain his health," she said.

She told Agata to go down to the Marina and tell Papa to come home. Tell him Camillo is home and is sick.

Mama saw to it that he was made to feel as comfortable as possible. Camillo went to his room as he was exhausted. Mama started preparing some food for him. She killed one of the chickens and made chicken soup.

Camillo's recovery was slow, it took months before he started to feel better and was able to get out of the house. As time went by he became stronger and decided to look for something to do. He found a job that he could do without it being too strenuous. It was cleaning large wine barrels with sea water. However, someone saw him working and reported him to the army. They recalled him to active duty and he had to leave and return to Catania. He was in Catania only a few months when he became ill again with the same illness. The doctor recommended that Camillo be given a medical discharge. He obtained his discharge papers and came home where Mama made sure he would regain his health.

It was morning and Camillo was eating his breakfast. We were happy he was home and we all gathered around him. Agata told Camillo about Leonardo, her fiancé. Leonardo and Agata were in love and very happy. Leonardo had a good job delivering telegrams and we were happy she had found a nice young man. One day a fishmonger friend of Papa's told him a lie about Leonardo. Pa believed him. He was very upset and told Agata he did not want her to have anything to do with Leonardo.

"Agata, I want you to break your engagement to Leonardo," said Pa.

"No! I love him and I don't want to break my engagement," said Agata.

My father was furious when she answered him back.

He said, "I am the Boss of this house. I don't want him to set one foot in my house."

He grabbed the broom and raised it to strike Agata. Mama was standing near Agata and she raised her arm in front of Agata to shield her. The handle came down and struck Mama's arm. Agata had no choice but to obey Papa and she broke the engagement. Leonardo's family was disappointed. They liked Agata and thought highly of our family. It wasn't very long after Agata had broken her engagement that she found out Papa's fishmonger friend had purposely lied about Leonardo. His daughter wanted Agata's fiancé for herself and the girl married Leonardo. Agata was heart broken. It was days before she came out of her room.

My father was old and he could not work. Camillo had to support the family and it was hard supporting all of us. Mama and Papa had given a lot of thought about Agata's and my future. We were the eldest of the girls, I was 17, and Agata was 20. There were few opportunities for jobs in Castellammare. They knew it would be better if Agata and I went to America. They wanted a better life for their daughters, so they decided that we should go. My three sisters were too young to come with us. They hoped that when we were in America, we would be able to send for them someday.

"Agata, Paolina, come here. Your father and I want to talk to you. You know your father and I have been thinking about sending you to America to live and we have decided to send you," said Ma.

"Ma, Pa. Are you sure we can go? Where will you get the money for the passage?" asked Agata.

"Yes, we have discussed it and we feel there is no future in Sicily for you," said Pa.

My parents went to friends and asked them to lend us the passage money. We were excited and my imagination was going wild. Everything I had heard about America, I believed. We heard everyone was rich in America that gold was on the streets. All you had to do was work hard and you could be anything you wanted to be. You could make a lot of money, even if it was just a few dollars a day. It was a good, new country where you had the opportunity to better your life. Going to America was like going to another planet. Ma went to the municipal building on Corso Garibaldi, in Castellammare and made all the arrangements for us.

We had to get ready; Agata and I started to pack our clothes in our suitcases and the large steamer truck Ma had bought for us.

The day before we left Castellammare, my sisters and I went down to bathe in the Vasca Della Regina.

"You're so lucky to be going to America. I'm so happy for you," said Rosina.

PAOLA'S REMEMBRANCES

"Write to us and tell us what America is like," said Francesca.

"I'm going to miss you," said little Annina.

We had a lot of fun playing in the water laughing and splashing each other. That was the last time we were all together in Sicily.

The sun shone through my bedroom window. Today was the day we were leaving for America. Rosina, Francesca and I got dressed and went downstairs. Ma had breakfast on the table; I was too excited to have anything but a cup of coffee. Ma got up from the table it was time to leave. We embraced and kissed my father, brother and sisters. It was very difficult saying good-bye, as they were not coming to see us off.

Ma, Agata and I took the train to Palermo. I had never been on a train before and it was strange hearing the constant sound of the wheels on the railroad tracks. The train pulled into the train station and we got off. Ma checked to see that our trunk was being delivered to the ship. When we arrived at the dock Ma went to the steamship office to have our visas stamped and we waited for her with our suitcases. I looked around at the people walking down the dock toward the small boat that would take us out to the ship.

"I wonder when Ma will return," I said.

"She's only been gone a little while, she'll be back soon," said Agata.

I turned around and I saw Ma coming toward us. She was carrying two small chairs.

"I bought these chairs for you so you can sit on the ship," said Ma.

Francesca Paolina Curatolo

"*Grazie*, Ma. Do you have our visas and passports?" Agata asked.

"Si, here they are. Be careful and don't lose them," said Ma.

Ma paid $50.00 each for our steerage class tickets. I heard the ship's whistle blow three times. It was time to say good-bye to my mother. Agata and I embraced and kissed her. We were all crying.

"Good-bye Mama, I love you," I said.

"Take care of yourselves, I love you both. Write to me when you arrive in America and let me know how you are," said Ma.

"We will," I said.

January 6, 1921 was the start of a new life for me. We departed from Palermo Sicily on the steamship Patria.

PAOLA'S REMEMBRANCES

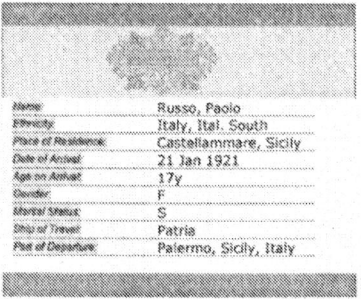

Passenger record from Ellis Island Archives
Note: Paola is the correct spelling of my name.

Francesca Paolina Curatolo

The Patria
Ship Image from the Archives of Ellis Island

CHAPTER SIX

I felt someone shaking me. It was my sister Agata. I don't know how long I had been standing staring out at the sea.

"Paolina, Paolina are you all right," asked Agata?

"Yes, I am going to miss Mama," I said.

Both of us stood at the ships railing and we could see our mother in the little boat as our ship set out for open water. She stayed there until she could not see the ship any more. My sister Anna told me that my mother did not get over the loss of her daughters. Years later my mother still cried for me and kept calling my name, Paolina. I would have sent for Mama but World War II prevented me from doing this.

I felt lost, as if there was nothing to hold onto ahead of me. But having my sister Agata with me made me feel better. Agata was two years older than I and when we came to America she said, "I will get married and that way you can stay with me."

Agata was like a mother to me now and we became very close, but I knew my life would never be the same. It was getting dark and we had to find where we were going to sleep. It took us a while before we found where we would be sleeping. The steerage passengers quarters were at the bottom of the ship. The room was open and iron framed beds were set in rows in the room. My bunk had a mattress filled with straw, covered with a coarsely woven canvas slipcover and I didn't have a blanket, or a pillow.

The second day on the ship, the sea became very rough. It started to storm and the rain poured down on the ship and the anger of the storm continued into the third day. I tried to eat but couldn't keep anything down. Everyone around me were seasick and the smell was unbearable. My mother had given us a bottle of Fernet Branca and told us to drink it if we got seasick. Fernet Branca is a very bitter liqueur. I took one swallow, but it was so bitter I couldn't drink it so we threw it away. The ship tossed and turned and the roar of the sea was almost too much to bear. The storm lessened and I felt a little better and tried to get up and walk, but it was impossible to stay upright for more than a minute. It started to rain harder and the ship tossed and turned. I became violently ill again and had to return to my bunk. Thank God, Agata was not as sick as I was. I stayed in my bed most of the 15 days that we were on board. People would pass by my bed and they would say to me, "You look like the Madonna." The smell of the food and people being sick made the atmosphere unbearable. The food was furnished by the steamship company and it wasn't very good.

There were many children on board the ship who had lice. They went to scratch their head and got a handful of lice. We'd watch as their mothers took care of them. Neither cleanliness, decency, nor comfort was possible. We were crowded into a small space. At night the crew would wash the decks where people had gotten sick. It was a long and painful journey. When I felt better I stayed on the deck, if the weather was good. The last day we were aboard the ship, I smelled something wonderful. Someone was roasting meat. Agata bought me a steak and I ate it with a slice of Italian bread. It tasted wonderful and I felt better.

The journey on the Patria was almost over. We knew we were getting close to land. Sea gulls were flying over the ship. People were rushing to the side of the ship looking for the Statue of Liberty. "There she is, look at her," they said, like it was a person who was greeting us. We have arrived in America! The journey was over.

CHAPTER SEVEN

We arrived in New York harbor on January 21, 1921 and the ship docked. Immigration inspectors and a medical officer, who examined the cabin class passengers, boarded the ship. Finally the steerage passengers were loaded onto a barge, destined for Ellis Island. We entered the baggage room where we left our possessions and then went into a large room with steps leading up to where the doctors and nurses examined us. People who were sick were sent to another part of Ellis Island.

Our ship was under quarantine and we had to stay on the island. My sister and I were not ill, but we spent 15 days quarantined on the Island. Agata and I were sent into a large room where we stayed until the quarantine was lifted.

One day we went for a walk around the outside of the building. "Paolina, look. What is that in the ocean?" asked Agata.

"I don't know," I said.

It was ice floating in the water. I had never seen ice before so I touched it. The people who worked on the island told us not to go near the water. The time we spent on Ellis Island seemed the longest waiting period for me.

"How many days do we have to be here?" people asked.

As for food, the steamship company was responsible for the cost of our meals while we were

PAOLA'S REMEMBRANCES

on the Island. I was very hungry since I had not eaten very much while on the ship. Breakfast included bread and tea, or coffee with milk and sugar. Dinner was soup, boiled meat and potatoes. The food was not very good. I couldn't eat the bread, our Italian bread was so delicious. I couldn't understand this kind of soft, mushy bread. I thought, what kind of bread do they eat in America? Thank God, I knew how to make my own bread.

Some of the inspectors spoke Italian and they asked us what our names were and where we would be staying and how we were going to make a living.

"My name is Paola Russo and we have relatives where will be staying," I said.

My sister told him, "I am called Agata Russo and we are going to get jobs in New York City."

The quarantine was over and we were released from the island.

"Paolina, are you ready? Let's go downstairs. We will be leaving soon," said Agata.

We collected our baggage and with our landing card prominently displayed, we followed the crowd of people going to the ferryboat on the next leg of our journey to our new life. It took us about thirty minutes to land at the dock. When we walked off the ferryboat I felt like a bird being let out of a cage. We walked into the customs room where they inspected our luggage. They marked an "X" on the top of our suitcases and we walked through the door. I felt like I was in a dream and so happy to be in America.

Mr. & Mrs. Navarra met us at the dock; they were friends of my parents. When they were visiting in Sicily my parents asked them if they would sponsor us and take care of us when we came to America.

The streets in New York City were crowded with horse drawn carts and street vendors selling clams and all kinds of food.

"Paolina, Agata! Come we will take you home," said Mr. Navarra.

Mr. & Mrs. Navarra's home was on Chrystie Street, about eight city blocks from the dock, so we walked to their apartment building.

"The apartment is in the next block," said Mrs. Navarra.

We turned the corner and I saw the apartment building. Mr. Navarra carried our baggage up the steps to the second floor. Our trunk was to be delivered later. He opened the door and took our suitcases into a bedroom.

"This is your bedroom. Make yourselves at home," said Mrs. Navarra.

The first thing we did when we arrived at the apartment after we unpacked was to write to our mother. I told her that we had arrived safely and we were well and happy. After a few days in New York City, Mrs. Navarra found work for us in a dress factory that was in the basement of the building we lived in. Two Jewish gentlemen owned the dress factory. I sewed buttons on dresses and my sister hemmed them. Our pay was $12.00 a week and we could not send my parents very much money, as we had to buy our food and pay the rent.

PAOLA'S REMEMBRANCES

It was a cold Saturday morning in New York City. We had our first week's pay, they paid us in cash, we were going shopping for winter coats, and I needed some shoes too. Coming from a tropical climate we did not have cold weather clothing. We stopped at a shoe store and I tried on a pair of shoes. They were brown leather and very attractive, the latest trend. The shoes laced up the front of my leg to the bottom of my knee. They made me feel and look very stylish.

Walking through the crowded immigrant neighborhood was like a visit to the old country. The streets were noisy open-air markets. Push carts lined the pavements, offering fruit, vegetables, poultry, fish, eggs, and any other thing you could think of—old coats for fifty cents, eyeglasses for thirty five cents, hats for a quarter, ribbons for a penny. Peddlers hawked their wares in a dozen different dialects, women wearing kerchiefs and shawls haggled for the best price. We finished our shopping and returned to the apartment.

Mrs. Navarra was waiting for us with her neighbor Anna, who turned out to be a neighbor of ours from Castellammare. Anna lived on the same street we lived on and we were happy to see her. We spent the afternoon visiting with Anna. It was nice talking about home, but Anna had to leave.

Mr. Navarra came home and told us that we were going to have a guest that evening. A friend of his, Albert Gance had come from Endicott, New York to visit his girl friend Palmina. Palmina told him she didn't want anything to do with him and broke their engagement. Albert was very upset and went to Mr. Navarra and told him what had happened. Mr. Navarra invited Albert to come to his home.

"Albert, two beautiful young girls have just arrived from Castellammare Del Golfo and are living with my wife and me. They come from a good family. Would you like to meet them?" asked Mr. Navarra.

"Yes. I would like that," said Albert.

It was 6:00 o'clock and the doorbell rang. Mrs. Navarra went to the door and let Albert in.

"Albert I would like you to meet Agata and Paolina Russo," said Mr. Navarra.

I was not interested in Albert, but Agata liked him. The evening went by quickly. It was time for Albert go to the train station and catch the Erie railroad train back to Endicott, New York. Albert came to New York City often to visit. One day Albert stopped by the apartment and Mr. Navarra told Albert that he had just lost his job.

"Since you're not working, come to Endicott, and you can start your own business selling fish," said Albert.

Mr. Navarra decided it would be for the best if they moved, as his wife was pregnant. They told us that they had decided to move to Endicott.

"Do you want to go with us?" asked Mrs. Navarra.

Agata and I discussed whether we should stay in New York City. We had been here three months so we decided to go with the Navarra's. We took the Erie railroad train to Endicott, where we got off at the station on North Street and walked down the

PAOLA'S REMEMBRANCES

train steps onto the train station platform. I looked around and I was disappointed in what I saw, it was desolate only a few houses. After living in New York City it was a shock to see how small this town was.

I turned to Albert and said, "Where did you bring us... to a cemetery?"

We moved into a house on Hill Avenue with Mr. & Mrs. Navarra. We had our own bedroom and shared expenses. One day Albert came to our house and invited us to come to his family's home. We were happy to meet our fellow countrymen from Castellammare, so we went. We met his mother, father, sisters Frances Monticello, and Angelina Gance, who was the same age as me. His brother Joseph owned a delicatessen store on the first floor of the house. Joseph and his wife, Petrina were gracious and kind to us. Albert's sister Angelina knew her way around Endicott and offered to show us around.

"I will help you find work," said Angelina.

She took us to the Endicott Johnson Shoe Factory employment office. We walked in the door and I looked around the room. There were a lot of people waiting to be called for their interviews. We sat down and patiently waited to be called. I was nervous because I couldn't speak English. Finally Mr. Costello, the interviewer called us into his office.

"What is your name?" he asked.

He didn't understand us when we told him our names.

"Tell him your name is Clara Russo." Angelina said to Agata.

I told him my name was Lena Russo. They gave us jobs and we started working the next day in the stitching room. I was slow doing my job because I was afraid. I felt alone; I did not know anyone and I felt as though everyone was watching me. It was difficult for me, but I worked hard.

Time went by and Agata and Albert became engaged. They were married and I was her maid-of-honor. Albert moved into the house we lived in. I had my own room. They were married for a few months when Agata started to have problems with her husband. Albert had his old girl friend Palmina from New York City on his mind and I felt bad for my sister. I went everywhere with my sister and Albert. Although there were times I didn't go with them I felt lost lonely and homesick for my family back in Castellammare. I tried to keep myself busy by going to the movies everyday which cost ten cents.

Albert and Agata and I decided to move from Hill Avenue and into an apartment on North Street, with Albert's brother Charlie Gance, his pregnant wife Maria Renda Gance and son Tony. Agata and Albert had their own room, but I didn't. I had to sleep on the couch. Shortly after we moved in the apartment Maria gave birth to another son Christopher.

PAOLA'S REMEMBRANCES

**Paola and Agata
We had been in America six months when this picture was taken.**

Francesca Paolina Curatolo

CHAPTER EIGHT

I met Tony, a young man from Sicily. Tony was thin, medium height dark brown hair and well dressed. Tony was infatuated with me and came to the house to see me often. He introduced me to his mother and brother and they also took a liking to me. After two or three months Tony and his family decided to have a big engagement party for me where he presented me with a diamond engagement ring. I thought to myself, he doesn't have a job, even though he has money and I didn't want to get involved with this man. I gave the engagement ring and the gifts his mother had given to me to my brother-in-law Albert.

"Albert, will you return the engagement ring to Tony and the gifts his mother gave me? I do not love him and don't want to be engaged to him let alone marry him," I said.

Albert took the ring and gifts back and gave them to Tony. Tony became furious. He did not like the fact that I had refused his marriage proposal. I avoided seeing Tony after I returned the engagement ring.

It was a very difficult time for me, as I remember hearing when I lived in Castellammare, of an incident that happened when a young girl rejected her suitor. It was the custom in the old country for the suitor to plot against the girl and abduct her. After she was taken and held for a period of time, she was let go. She was in disgrace and had no choice but to accept the suitors proposal.

My sister Agata and her husband Albert and I moved from the North Street apartment to a rooming house on Oak Hill Avenue run by a woman called Betsy Bennette. We rented two bedrooms and had the use of the kitchen. All the tenants shared the bathroom. I had my own bedroom, but I didn't have a bed, so I slept on the trunk my mother had bought for us when we left Castellammare.

Agata and I walked to work every day. Near the factory was a doughnut shop, I loved doughnuts and I'd stop to buy one. A few months passed by and working hard at my job when I became ill. I was very weak and I couldn't go to work. Agata didn't know what to do so she sent me to live with a friend of ours, Maria Aliva who had lived on the same street in Castellammare. Maria now lived in Susquehanna, Pennsylvania.

Maria called the doctor and he examined me, but couldn't find anything wrong. The doctor tried to encourage me. He knew I was homesick and depressed and he told me to be happy. I missed my homeland and my family especially my mother. My sister was married and I was happy for her, but I felt all alone.

Maria took good care of me and I started to feel better. I lived with her for a month and then returned home to Endicott. When I saw my sister I ran to her and kissed her. I was happy to see her and she was happy to have me back.

CHAPTER NINE

One day while I was working in the stitching room of the Endicott Johnson factory an Italian woman Maria Curatolo Barone came over to me and introduced herself and we became friends. She had come to Endicott to visit her sister Francesca Renda. Maria knew I was not married and she decided to play matchmaker. Un-be-knownst to me she decided to write to her brother Calogero, who was not married and living in New York City.

She wrote, "Calogero, there is a girl here in Endicott that I want you to meet, come right away."

When Calogero arrived in Endicott they described me to him and told him where I would be the next morning. It was early morning Agata and I started walking down Oak Hill Avenue. We stopped in front of the factory on North Street where Calogero was waiting for me. I looked at him and he looked at me, we didn't speak. Later he told me when he saw my big brown eyes he fell in love with me instantly.

Calogero applied for a job at the Endicott Johnson Shoe factory located on North Street. He knew how to operate a sewing machine as he'd been working in a dress factory in New York City sewing beads on dresses. He got the job and started working the next day in the vamping room. Every day after he had finished his work, Calogero would come to the stitching room where I was working, sit

PAOLA'S REMEMBRANCES

next to my machine and cut the thread that held the shoes together. I knew he liked me, but I did not care for him and didn't have any intention of becoming involved with him.

One day my friend Angelina Aliva came to me and asked me if I would like to go out with Calogero. I said no. . . I don't want to go out with anyone! Angelina went to Calogero and told him she asked me if I would go out with him and that I had said no. Calogero was so unhappy that he cried himself to sleep on the back steps of his apartment.

It was Friday when Angelina Aliva came to me to have a heart to heart talk. She warned me that I was in danger and she said, do you know what happens to a girl who refuses a marriage proposal? This is about to happen to you. Go and talk to Calogero, he loves you and will take care of you .

I went to see Calogero and we talked. We decided to elope and made plans to meet at the taxi stand on Monroe Street. Before getting to the taxi stand I stopped at the 5 and 10 cent store and bought myself a pink ribbon. I was just an innocent young girl and wanted something pretty to take with me. I didn't tell anyone what I was going to do, not even my sister Agata. Calogero was waiting for me and we took a taxi to Binghamton, New York. He took me to his hotel room where he offered me rigatoni with sauce that he had cooked on a hot plate for me. I didn't want any, as I was nervous, so he ate by himself. We stayed three days in the hotel and then Calogero's brother-in-law, Vincenzo Renda picked us up and brought us back to Endicott.

Francesca Paolina Curatolo

I went away with Calogero because I wanted protection and security. Calogero was an honorable man and he respected and loved me very much and I knew he would take care of me. I did not love him when we went to Binghamton, but I did grow to love him after we were married. We stayed on Squires Avenue with Calogero's older brother Pietro, his wife Giuseppina and Joseph their baby son.

On December 16, 1922, Father Rocco Macchiavena in Saint Anthony's Roman Catholic Church married Calogero and me in a private ceremony. I was nineteen and Calogero was twenty five years old. I wore a simple dress and Calogero a suit. Pietro, my husband's brother, was our best man and his wife Giuseppina was my matron of honor. After the wedding ceremony the four of us went to our friends at the Mistretta's house. Calogero and I walked in the front door and into the living room. In the corner of the room was a table filled with food. The Mistrettas had prepared a wedding celebration for us. The phonograph was playing and we danced. I felt awkward, I didn't know how to dance. It was getting dark and it was time to go home.

We lived with Pietro and Giuseppina on Squires Avenue for three months when the apartment upstairs became available and were happy that we were moving into our own apartment. A few months passed by when Calogero surprised me with a beautiful diamond ring that had thirteen smaller diamonds on either side of the center diamond. I was pleased I knew he worked hard saving his money to buy it.

Calogero was born on September 24, 1898, in Castellammare Del Golfo, Sicily to Guiseppe Curatolo and Leonarda Messina Curatolo.

His father Guiseppe had one brother, Antonio. His mother Leonarda had eight brothers, Antonio, Francesco, Guiseppe, Girolamo, Camillo, Paolo, Calogero and Gaspare and one sister Maria. His paternal grandparents were Pietro Curatolo and Francesca Curatolo, and his maternal grandparents were Calogero Messina and Maria Messina. Calogero had two brothers: Pietro and Antonio and three sisters, Francesca, Maria and Anna.

Calogero came to the United States December 18, 1913 at the age of 16 on the ship Princess Irene. He worked in New York City in a dress factory. Calogero had relatives who lived in Brooklyn, New York and they introduced him to Palmina Oddo my sister-in-law Peppina's sister who taught him how to read and write Italian. He taught himself how to read and write English. He attended night school at the George W. Johnson (North Side) School in Endicott, NY. and he received a certificate of Literacy signed by Charles D. Knapp, examiner and H. H. Crumb, Superintendent of Schools, dated March 1931. Calogero became a citizen of the United States on January 6, 1931 when he was thirty-three years old. This was a very happy day for him.

Francesca Paolina Curatolo

Paola and Calogero Curatolo

CHAPTER TEN

Some time had passed and my sister Agata came to see us at our apartment. She pretended that she was upset with me and had to act this way because her husband was making it difficult for her because I had run off with Calogero. A month after my marriage, I had a visit from her husband and his two brothers. They were angry with me because their sister Angelina had eloped and they said that I had made the comment that I wouldn't have done such a thing. They thought I was criticizing their sister.

"I do not remember saying this," I said.

They didn't believe me and they were trying to make trouble for me.

Pietro, my husband's brother was there. He told them, "I don't care if she said it or not. Get out of my house."

They left the house and did not bother me again.

Agata became pregnant and gave birth to a son, Anthony. I was pregnant with my oldest daughter Leona when she gave birth to Tony. Agata and Albert had another baby, a son Melchiore who became ill with meningitis. They were devastated when Melchiore died at the age of seven months. The loss of her son, had taken its toll on Agata, but when she found out that she was pregnant again it made her happy and looking forward to the birth of her baby. Agata gave birth to a daughter, Rosalie.

Agata became ill and was in the hospital. Her husband wanted to take Rosie to see her so he brought her to me and I got her ready. I dressed her in one of the pretty dresses her mother had made for her and curled her hair with a curling iron in the Shirley Temple style. Rosie was a beautiful child and when she walked into the hospital room her mother was surprised and happy to see her. She was her pride and joy. Rosie and her father left the hospital and on their way to my house when they stopped at Albert's brother, Joe's store. Joe gave Rosie chocolate candy and she got it all over herself. Rosie walked in the door with her face and dress covered with chocolate. I was upset with Albert for letting her get the chocolate all over herself.

My sister and her children came to our home often. We were very close and the children enjoyed being with my family. Rosie and Tony liked eating my freshly baked bread.

"Why are you eating here and you will not eat at home," asked their mother?

"Aunt Paolina makes delicious bread," said Rosie.

My sister is no longer with us and I miss her very much. Rosie calls me every day to see how I am. She is like a daughter to me and I love her very much.

Agata, Rosie and Tony Gance

CHAPTER ELEVEN

Leona was born in our home September 1923. I had a difficult time giving birth and the doctor thought I was going to die. She called an associate, Doctor Fossberry who came to our home and gave me a shot. It took a while before I started feeling better. Calogero and I were very happy with our beautiful daughter. She looked like a little doll. My husband's fellow workers surprised me with a beautiful baby blanket and clothes.

When Leona was four months old I decided to go back to work. I asked Giuseppina my sister-in-law, if she would take care of Leona while I was at work and she said she would. When I returned to the factory I found I did the work faster as I had more confidence. Every morning when I left my baby she would cry. She didn't want me to leave her. It became harder and harder every day leaving her. One day she cried so hard she wouldn't let me go. That was the day I decided to quit my job and stay home. I enjoyed staying home and I was very happy taking care of my family.

My sister came to my home to visit me more often and we'd take our babies out for a stroll in the baby carriages. Calogero and I moved to Watson Blvd., when our daughter was two years old and I gave birth to our second child, Joseph. I was very happy and I would sing as I cleaned and cooked also I worked hard making all my children's clothes and taking care of my family.

Calogero's sister Anna and her husband Antonio Lauricella bought a house at 205 North McKinley Avenue in Endicott. They lived in the downstairs apartment and we moved into the apartment upstairs. Our children Melchiore, Anna, Francesca and Agata were born while we lived in this home. Each time we had a baby the Endicott Johnson Corporation gave a gift of twenty silver dollars, ten for the baby, along with a pair of baby shoes, and ten silver dollars for me.

My husband and I had six beautiful children and I am very proud of them.

Anna and Tony Lauricella sold us the house on McKinley Avenue. My husband had property that he sold to Tony and he used that property as a down payment on the house. Calogero went to a private moneylender for the remainder of the money to purchase the house. He was very punctual in making his payments each month and he paid the house in full.

Next to our home on North McKinley Avenue, was the Bonner Memorial Presbyterian Church. The church was an Italian Mission Church. I could hear the people singing hymns in Italian and I learned them all. I had been told not to go into the Protestant Church because they did not do the right things and they were bad. Calogero and I with our four children had been attending St. Anthony's Roman Catholic Church. Leona, Joseph and Melchiore had been baptized in the Roman Catholic Church when they were babies, but Annie

Francesca Paolina Curatolo

was three years old and she had not been baptized so I wrote to my half brother Girolamo who lived in Detroit Michigan, and asked if he would be her Godfather. He agreed and came to Endicott with his wife, and daughters Virginia, and Nancy. After the baptism we had a party at our house with our relatives and friends.

One day I decided to see for myself what was going on in the Protestant Church. Rev. Oscar Vitale was the preacher and I heard him talking about God and Jesus. He said that Jesus walked everywhere, in the streets and the mountains preaching the evangelical message, about God's love. My mother had told me the same thing. I knew what Rev. Vitale was preaching was true. I believed what he preached and I started to go to church every Sunday. I learned more about God and Jesus from the Bible, as I could understand the message and because it was being preached in my native language, Italian. In the Catholic Church the Mass was spoken in Latin.

As my children grew up I sent Leona, Joe, Melchiore and Annie to Sunday school. After Sunday school, they'd attend church service with my husband and me. Anna and Tony Lauricella and a close friend, John Ciaozzo, had been attending church services before we did. Pietro's children also started attending church services. I remember at Christmas time all my children learned Christmas poems and they recited them in the Christmas pageant. Francie and Agatina were four and two when they started Sunday school. They learned Bible verses that I taught them and they recited them on Sunday to the Sunday school teacher. Francie and Agatina brought home posters of Jesus with the verses they had memorized written on the back and they were so happy. This is one of the Bible verses that my children memorized.

"For God so loved the world, that he gave is only begotten Son, that whosoever believeth in him should not perish, but have everlasting life."

John 3;16.

My children also learned these prayers.

"Dear Father, bless this food we take and bless us all for Jesus sake."

Amen.

"Now I lay me down to sleep, I pray the Lord my soul to keep. If I should die before I wake, I pray the Lord my soul to take, and this I ask for Jesus sake."

Amen.

Calogero, and I became members of Bonner along with all my children. They all sang in the church choir and taught Sunday school.

My sister and her husband did not look with favor, my belonging to a Protestant church. Our fellow countrymen did not approve of us joining the *Protestante*. It was not easy living in the Italian community.

Francesca Paolina Curatolo

Leona, Joseph and Melchiore Curatolo

CHAPTER TWELVE

I would like to tell you about our children as they were growing up. When Leona, Joe, Menzie and Annie started going to school, they did not speak English. I spoke Sicilian to them, my native tongue. As my children learned the English language they taught it to me.

Leona was an obedient child. She was around thirteen years old when I had given birth to my daughter Agata. While I was in the hospital she took care of the children and the housework with the help of my sister-in-law Anna.

"Pa, will you give me some money? I want to buy some new kitchen curtains, so the house will look nice when Mama comes home from the hospital," said Leona.

My husband gave her the money and Leona went to the store and bought the curtains. It was time for me to leave the hospital and was waiting for Calogero to come to take me home. I missed the children and was anxious to see them. When I walked in the door with the baby they gathered around us. They were excited and happy to have me home. I complemented Leona on how clean the house was and how pretty the new kitchen curtains were.

Joe was a quiet boy, but he was mischievous at times. Joe became ill when he was two years old with a high fever. We called the Endicott Johnson

Francesca Paolina Curatolo

Medical and they sent a Japanese doctor to our home. I do not recall the doctor's name. The Endicott Johnson Corporation had free medical service for all their employees.

"Mr. & Mrs. Curatolo, your son has meningitis," said the Doctor.

When I heard this I didn't know what to do and was afraid Joe was going to die. The doctor gave us instructions and prescribed medication and said he'd return in a few days to see how Joe was.

Joey kept saying to the doctor "boo-boo," and the doctor said, yes you have a boo-boo.

I cried and prayed that Joey would be all right, he did start feeling better. Joe recovered from meningitis, but he was very weak.

Melchiore, we called him Menzie had a hard head, *testa dura*. He was very stubborn and there were times he would not listen to me. There was this one time I thought I heard him saying something bad.

"Menzie I don't want to hear you say that again," I said.

I took my shoe off and I threw it in his direction.

"Menzie pick my shoe up and bring it to me," I said.

He would not pick my shoe up, so I picked it up and put it in his hand and told him to give it to me. He would not give it to me and I became so angry with him I started to spank him.

"Stop! What are you trying to do kill him?" asked my husband.

I was so frustrated I started to cry. Taking care of six children at times was overwhelming. I love my children and I didn't spank them for every little thing they did wrong but I spanked them when it was important so they would understand what they were doing was wrong. My son later told me he remembered this occasion and he had not used the word I thought he had.

He said, "If I had picked up the shoe and brought it to you, you would have spanked me again."

He was right. I thought he was using bad language and I was trying to teach him right from wrong. I know now I did not hear what I thought I heard and I feel very bad that I spanked him.

One day Peppina my sister-in-law told me she had seen Joe and Menzie climbing down the front porch on the rose trellis, they were around ten and twelve years old. She lived on Roosevelt Avenue and she could see our house from her back yard. I became upset and I went to Joe and Menzie and told them that I found out they had been climbing down the trellis.

"You can hurt yourself climbing down the rose trellis," I said.

My brother Camillo came to America December 1, 1923 at the age of 24 on the ship Dante Alighieri and stayed with my family. He got a job at Endicott Johnson in the West Endicott Factory. Camillo sent part of his pay back to Ma and Pa who were old now and needed financial help and he helped us by paying for his room and board. Camillo was a wonderful, thoughtful, considerate brother and he was kind to my children. Saturday nights he went to the Concordia Society Lodge to play cards and when my children saw him going out the door they asked him to bring home Chocolate and gum. He'd bring them candy and gum when he won at cards.

"*Zio* Millo, please bring us chocolate, and chewing gum," the children asked.

Sunday morning the children ran to Camillo, and asked him, "Did you bring us chocolate, and chewing gum?"

"Yes, here you are," he said.

They were so happy when he gave them the Hershey bars and chewing gum.

One day Menzie and Joe were outside playing when they came in the house and went in their room to play. They were hiding under their bed and I knew they were up to something. I looked under the bed and I saw Joe's blond curly hair caught on the springs.

"Joe, Menzie come on out. What are you doing under there?" I asked.

They wouldn't come out. I tried to get them to come out by getting a broom, and prying them out from under the bed but they wouldn't come out. I finally pulled them out and I gave them a swat on their bottom. Hiding under their bed was one of the places they liked to hide from me.

Salvatore, my half brother came to Endicott from Detroit Michigan for a visit and he decided to stay. He got a job as a maintenance man at the North Side Park on Oak Hill Avenue. Endicott Johnson owned the park. Everyone liked Sam. He took care of the Merry-go-round and park grounds. When the swimming pool was open he made sure the children were safe.

PAOLA'S REMEMBRANCES

Joe was 12 years old when he started taking violin lessons. His violin teacher Mr. Mayberry came to our home in the afternoon to give him a lesson.

Joe didn't want to take lessons, but Salvatore persuaded him to take them.

"Joe, I will give you 10 cents if you take the violin lesson," said Sam.

"All right I'll do it, but I don't like playing the violin, Uncle Sam," said Joe.

Sometimes we would sing along while he played his violin and he would get mad.

"Stop! I can't play when you are singing," said Joe.

Joe's lesson was over and Mr. Mayberry was leaving. I paid him fifty cents for the lessons. Sometimes I'd give him a loaf of hot homemade bread that I had just taken out of the oven.

We had finished our supper and the children were doing their homework. I told them when they were through to come into the living room where Calogero and I were listening to the news on the radio. Leona came in the living room and sat down.

"We finished our homework," said Leona.

The Amos and Andy program was just coming on. Francie and Agatina sat on the floor in front of the radio. Joe, Menzie and Annie sat on the sofa. The program was over and it was time for bed.

It was 8:00 o'clock in the morning and it was time for the children to go to school. Joe met his friends, and they walked to the Henry B. Endicott Junior High School on Jackson Avenue. I went back into the house and started my housework.

At noon the children would be coming home to eat their lunch. They had an hour for lunch so I had it ready for them. I had just made some bread and was taking it out of the oven when they came into the kitchen.

"Sit down and eat," I said. "I made pasta with peas and bread for you."

They quickly finished eating lunch and hurried back to school.

It was three thirty and I was outside waiting for the children to come home from school. Some of Joe's friends came to me and told me that Joe had returned late to school that afternoon. When Joe walked in the door I confronted him.

"Why were you late going back to school?" I asked.

I was ready to slap him, but before I could, he surprised me.

"Here, I bought this for you," he said.

It was a box of face powder.

"I was late because I was helping a man who was selling things," said Joe.

There were vendors on North Street by IBM who sold goods. Joe wanted to buy a present for me as it was going to be Mother's Day. I was surprised, as I didn't expect him to do this for me. I was pleased with his thoughtfulness.

Annie was an easygoing child and she made friends easily. One day Sarah Caiozzo's mother Viola came to my house looking for Sarah.

"Mrs. Curatolo, is Sarah here?" asked Viola.

"No, she is not and Annie is not home. They must be together," I said.

Annie came home and I asked her to come in the kitchen.

"Annie, where were you? What have you been doing?" I asked.

"I was with Sarah and we went to a friend's house," said Annie.

"You didn't tell me and I was worried," I said.

I spanked her, but she didn't cry. Annie knew she should not have gone off without telling me.

"You are not to go anywhere without telling me," I said.

Annie was always tagging along with her older brother Menzie. On this one particular day they were outside playing when the driver of a Pearl Bakery truck drove up. He parked the truck near Saint Casimir's Church, got out and started delivering bread. Annie and Menzie saw the parked truck, ran across the street and sat down on the running board. The driver didn't know that they were sitting on the running board when he returned and he started driving away. Menzie and Annie both fell off the running board. Annie screamed as her right hand went under the truck's wheel. The truck stopped and the driver got out to see what had happened, but Annie and Menzie had gotten up and ran home.

"Ma, Annie hurt her hand. We were sitting on the running board of the bakery truck and the truck run over her hand," said Menzie.

Annie was crying. Her hand was swollen and dirty.

"Menzie, are you all right?" I asked.

"Yes. I'm okay," he said.

"Menzie, go and ask Mrs. Vitale to call a taxi for us," I said.

The Vitales were the only people in our neighborhood who had a telephone. When the taxi came Annie was screaming and kicking and wouldn't get into the cab I had to push her into the taxi. Mrs. Vitale came with us to the Medical. The doctor checked her hand, it was badly bruised, but not broken. He put ointment on her hand, wrapped it with gauze and gave me medicine. When we came home the bread man was waiting for us because he was so worried. He was glad Annie was all right and not badly injured. When he left he gave us some bread.

Francie was a sensitive child easily frightened and she cried all the time. I had to take her to the doctors often, as she was sickly and fainted easily.

Paul Lauricella, (the nephew of my brother-in-law Tony Lauricella) and Francie were outside playing. Francie had a stick in her hand and Paul tried to take the stick away from her and she would not let it go.

"Give me the stick," said Paulie.

"No. I want it!" said Francie.

Paulie and Francie kept pulling back and forth on the stick. Paulie let go of the stick and it hit her in the stomach. Francie fell to the ground.

"*Zia* Paolina, Francie hurt herself," cried Paulie.

I heard Paulie yelling for me and ran outside to see Francie on the ground where she had fainted. I picked her up and blew air into her face to revive her. She came around and I carried her into the house.

There were many times Francie got hurt. One time I had finished waxing the kitchen floor and she walked through the kitchen and slid on the waxed floor. She hit the back of her head on the kitchen radiator and was knocked unconscious. I thought she was dead and started to cry. I picked her up and tried to revive her, but I couldn't. I was frightened and tried blowing in her face, but didn't have enough breath as I was crying so hard. My husband and Rev. Oscar Vitale along with Annina, my sister-in-law, were outside the house talking heard me crying. They quickly came upstairs to see what was wrong. I was holding Francie in my arms and Annina grabbed Francie out of my arms.

"Paolina give her to me," said Annina.

Annina put cold water on her face and blew air into Francie and revived her.

We had a cast iron cooking stove in our kitchen and on one side of the stove there was a section where the wood ashes fell. I had finished baking bread and the oven was still hot. Francie was playing near it and she did not know that the oven was hot and touched it. I heard her screaming and I ran to her and saw the skin on her hands was blistered. I didn't know what to do except put butter on them and wrapped cloth around them. We called a taxi and took her to the Medical on Washington Avenue. The doctor examined Francie's hands and told us they were not severe burns and in a few days her hands would be better.

He put ointment on them and wrapped them with gauze and we went home.

Agatha, we called her Agatina, my youngest daughter was a bright child, quick to learn and an even-tempered child. When she was seven months old she could walk by herself. At the age of one I started to potty train her. I put her on the toilet and I sat next to her holding her. She was so small I was afraid that she would fall into the toilet. Agatina started talking at one and a half. She was hungry and wanted her bottle. I put the bottle in her mouth and she pulled it out.

"Ma *salata*, (salty)" said Agatina.

"That's not possible," I said.

Agatina knew the difference between sugar and salt. I took the bottle from her and tasted the milk. She was right it was salty.

Agatina was eager to learn how to write and I taught her when she was three. She wrote all over the front sidewalk the names of her Godparents, Elodia and Joseph Tedeschi and their children. I took her to sign up for kindergarten, but they would not let her start school as they felt she was too young so she started school at the age of four. Agatina was an excellent student. Her report card was full of gold stars.

PAOLA'S REMEMBRANCES

Joseph, Melchiore, Leona, Anna, Francesca, Paola, Agata and Calogero Curatolo

Francesca Paolina Curatolo

Melchiore and Joseph Curatolo

CHAPTER THIRTEEN

Every Saturday I cleaned the entire house. I had finished waxing the kitchen floor and was getting ready to go to a wedding shower for Josephine Coppola when I slid across the floor and hit my head on the baseboard of the kitchen wall.

"Mama are you all right," asked Menzie?

Francie, Agatina and Leona saw me fall, but they could not help me. I couldn't move. My son Menzie picked me up and put me on my bed.

"Mama, do you want us to call the Doctor?" asked Francie.

"No, I will be all right. I just want to rest," I said.

I started to feel a little better and I put my feet over the side of the bed. I started to stand, but I couldn't. I was dizzy and had to go back to bed.

"Mama, I think we should call the Doctor," said Menzie.

"No, I will stay in bed and will feel better soon. Leona, you and your sisters go to the shower and tell Josie what happened," I said.

The girls went to the shower and conveyed my regrets. It took me a few days to recover from my fall.

Every Saturday night I'd bathe the children and I'd wrap Francie, Agatina and Annie's hair with strips of cotton cloth, making them into banana curls. Sunday morning, before we went to church

Francesca Paolina Curatolo

I'd comb the girl's hair out into the style of Shirley Temple's curls and dressed them in their Sunday dresses I made for them. My husband bought blue suits for the boys that cost twelve dollars each and they wore them on Sunday. Everyone complimented me on how well dressed my children were.

I sent the children off to Sunday school and finished preparing our noon meal. Everything was ready before we went to church. On the stove was spaghetti sauce with chunks of meat and meatballs and in the oven, I had a chicken baking. All I had to do after church service was to put a pot of water on the stove to cook the pasta.

After church Elodia and Joseph Tedeschi and their children Remo, Romolo and Joseph (we called him Dino) came over to our home. Calogero offered Compare Tedeschi a glass of homemade wine. I remember Romolo and Remo dipping pieces of bread into the spaghetti sauce and tasting the roasted chicken. After dinner we would go over to their home. We spent many wonderful Sunday afternoons together.

Compare had a grocery store on the corner of Washington Avenue and North Street. He had ordered a train carload of grapes and had it delivered to our house. Calogero, Joe, Menzie and my brother Camillo made wine in our cellar for Compare Tedeschi. They used a wine press that he had given us and than we stored the wine in our cellar in large wooden wine barrels. When the wine was ready for drinking Calogero gave Compare Tedeschi half of the wine he made.

It was evening and I was cooking pasta with *cicoria* (chicory) when I heard a knock at the kitchen door. It was my Commare Elodia and her son Dino. We were happy to see them and I asked them to join us at the supper table.

"Come on in and have some pasta with *cicoria*," I said.

Whenever I was making pasta with *cicoria*, Commare and Dino happened to show up at our house. It was a coincidence and we teased her because we knew she liked it.

Commare Elodia encouraged me to go to night school. She knew I wanted to become a citizen of the United States. I learned to read and write English and about the constitution, the Presidents, and the divisions of the government. I passed the examination and I appeared before the Judge of the U. S. District Court Department of Immigration and Naturalization on January 4, 1944. This was a happy day for me. I am proud to be a citizen of the United States. Mrs. Sarah Vitale and Elodia Tedeschi were my witnesses.

CHAPTER FOURTEEN

Our family and Pietro's family always spent the holidays together. We alternated celebrating Thanksgiving, Christmas and Easter at our homes. Anna and Tony Lauricella also celebrated with us. Christmas was a happy time around our home. Calogero and the children helped me prepare for the holiday. We made all different kinds of Italian cookies. Christmas Eve was a special time for us. My husband helped me make homemade macaroni and the children helped too.

"Ma, what are we having for Christmas dinner?" asked Francie.

"We are going to have chicken soup, homemade macaroni, sausage, brasciole, meatballs and pieces of veal, beef, pork, in meat sauce, baked ham, baked chicken and salad," I said.

"I can't wait for Christmas to come," said Francie.

"Children it is time to decorate the Christmas tree. Your father just put it in the living room," I said.

Agatina and Francie ran into the living room they were excited and wanted to help their brothers and sisters trim the tree.

"Ma, can we pop some popcorn, so we can put it on the tree?" asked Leona.

Calogero put strings of lights on the tree and the children strung the popcorn and paper chains on the tree. They finished decorating the tree with brightly colored ornaments and tinsel. The tree looked beautiful.

"Francie, Agatina come. It's time to take your baths and go to bed," I said.

"We have to finish wrapping the Christmas presents," said Francie.

"All right when you're done, put the presents under the tree and let me know when you're ready to take your baths," I said.

Everything was ready for Christmas day and I finally was able to get to sleep. I was sleeping soundly when I heard something. It was Agatina.

"Mama, did Santa Claus come yet?" she asked.

"No, not yet. Go back to bed. I will let you know when he does," I said.

I put her back into bed, covered her and then checked Francie and Annie. Leona, Joe and Menzie were asleep so I went back to bed. I had a big day ahead of me with all the relatives coming over for Christmas.

It was 5 o'clock in the morning and I awoke to the sound of giggling. I turned in the bed and nudged my husband.

"Calogero, wake up. The children are up and they want to open their presents," I said.

We got out of bed and I looked out of the bedroom window to see snow on the ground. The children would be happy, as they had been wishing we would get some snow for Christmas. I walked into the kitchen where they were sitting at the kitchen table waiting for us.

"Merry Christmas Mama, Papa! Can we open our Christmas presents?" they asked.

"Merry Christmas, let's go into the living room and see what Santa Claus brought you," I said.

We couldn't afford to get very much for them, but they were happy with what they received.

"Joe, Menzie this is your present," said Calogero.

The boys tore the paper from the box.

"Look what we got — a train set! Thank you, Mama and Papa," they said.

Calogero and the boys started to set the train up. Leona and Annie were pleased with the dresses I had made for them and Francie and Agatina played with their dolls.

"It's time to put your things away. Your cousins will be here soon and we have to get ready for our company," I said.

They put their gifts away and went into the bedroom to get dressed. Joe and Menzie were dressed and playing with the train. The girls came out of their room and started setting the table in the living room, which accommodated eighteen people. There was a knock at the door and Annie went to see who was there. It was my nieces Leona, Sarah and Francie.

"Merry Christmas," they said.

"Come in Merry Christmas!" said Annie.

"Where is the rest of your family?" I asked.

"They will be here in a few minutes," said Leona.

They went into the living room and put the presents under the Christmas tree.

PAOLA'S REMEMBRANCES

Agatina and Francie exchanged presents with cousin Fran. The rest of the family had arrived and they went into the living room. Dinner was ready and I called everyone to come and sit down so Calogero could say grace before we started eating. On the table was antipasto, which consisted of provolone cheese, Genoa hard salami, capocollo, pepperoni, black and green Italian olives and sliced melon wrapped in prosciutto. Leona helped me serve the first course chicken soup and then the rest of the meal. Everyone complimented me on how delicious the food was. The girls helped me clear the dishes from the table so we could sit around it and visit the rest of the afternoon. Francie and Agatina opened the presents Francie had brought and then they played with their toys.

Some of the older children fell asleep on the couch because they had eaten so much food. Later that afternoon the Tedeschis dropped by and brought each of my children a silver dollar and a present for Agatina, their Godchild and one for Francie, too. They never forgot to bring Francie a gift when they brought one to Agatina. The girls were close in age and they didn't want Francie to feel left out. It was getting dark outside and our guests were leaving. The children had a long day and were tired and ready for bed.

It was dark outside when I woke up. Calogero was already up and on his way out the door. He had to catch the bus to work. I checked to see if the children were up, but they were sleeping. I got dressed and started cleaning the living room. The children heard me and got up to help me put away the tables and chairs we used for Christmas dinner. They didn't have to go to school so after breakfast they went outside to play in the snow. I looked at the clock and it was time for lunch. The children had been out playing and it was time for them to come in. I looked out the window, they were making snow angels in the snow and their faces were red from the cold. I called to them to come in the house. They were full of energy and didn't want to stop playing, but I insisted they come in and change their wet clothes. They put on dry clothes and came into the kitchen and sat down at the table. I had prepared chicken soup and some freshly baked bread.

New Years had come and gone and the children were eager to return to school except for Francie. She couldn't go because she had a stomach ache and I had to keep her home. She later told me she was afraid of school and the teachers. She didn't know how to cope. Francie was in the second grade when she came down with rheumatic fever and had to stay in bed for about half of the year. She started to get better and was able to sit up in a chair. We brought her outside to get some fresh air. It took awhile before she was better.

Easter Sunday was here and the smell of spring was in the air. It was a warm sunny day and the children were dressed in their new Easter clothes anxious for Sunday school to start. They went out the back door, ran over to the church and down the stairs where Sunday School was about to start. They were anxious because they knew the Sunday School staff was going to give them their Easter baskets. Sunday School was over and they came upstairs to the sanctuary and sat next to Calogero and me. Their faces had big smiles on them as they showed me their yellow and green Easter baskets. I looked around the church and it was filling up with people. The women looked bright and springlike, wearing their new Easter hats. Easter service began with the choir singing as they walked down the church aisle. Reverend Vitale gave an inspiring Easter message. After church the Tedeschis stopped at our house and brought my children frozen ice cream in the shape of little chicks, and a bottle of Virginia Dare wine for me. When they left we went to Pietro's house for Easter dinner. They had enough food on the table to last us all day, it was a joyous and wonderful day.

CHAPTER FIFTEEN

School was out and vacation time was here. Calogero's cousins Frances and Thomas Spinosa invited us to spend our two week summer vacation with them in Brooklyn. The children, Calogero and I took the train to Brooklyn.

"Come in! we are happy to see you, how was the trip?" asked Frances.

We were happy to be there after our long train ride. Tommy took our suitcases and put them into our room.

Mary and her husband Leo will be coming over this evening to see you, said Tommy.

Mary D'Angelo and Frances Spinosa and their brother Peter were Curatolos and my husband's cousins. Calogero had other relatives living in Brooklyn and they invited us to their homes for dinner every night of the week we were there. We enjoyed our vacation in Brooklyn visiting with them all. It was nice having time off from my everyday cooking and cleaning.

We took turns spending summer vacations visiting each other's homes. I recall Frances and Thomas coming to our home in Endicott with their children, and Frances's mother Zia Francesca Curatolo. Frances's brother Peter and sister Mary and her husband Leo also visited us. When the relatives came to Endicott they always stayed in our house and brought us a big tray of Italian cookies and a large basket full of lobster, clams, snails and different kinds of fresh seafood packed in ice. Pietro's family came to our house when the Brooklyn relatives were in town and they joined us for dinner. Frances gave them some Italian cookies and Pietro invited all of us over to his house for supper the next day. The relatives enjoyed being in the country, as it was a change from city life.

It was a warm August night and supper was over. We were outside sitting on the front porch of the house when we saw a fire burning on a hill near Hayes Avenue.

"I wonder what is going on," said Menzie?

We could see crosses burning with people wearing white hooded robes standing around them.

"Never mind it's not our business, let's go in the house," I said.

Later we found out these people were called the Ku Klux Klan — K.K.K.

The Klan organizers selected Binghamton as their state headquarters in 1920. A variety of social tensions were largely responsible for the growth of the Klan in the city and in the urban areas. In its sixth year of activity in the Binghamton area the Ku Klux Klan never became a dominant force.

One of the reasons for the Klan's failure in Binghamton was the Klan decided to air its grievances with George F. Johnson out in the open. The thousands of workers, merchants and politicians, who depended on the industrialist, were outraged.

We did not know who these people in the Klan were and we didn't want to know. Whenever we

saw the crosses burning on the hill we would go inside the house and close the door.

PAOLA'S REMEMBRANCES
CHAPTER SIXTEEN

Thanksgiving was over and we were getting ready for the Christmas holiday. It was 1940 and World War II had started. I remember hearing on the radio that the Japanese had attacked Pearl Harbor. Those were unhappy times as everyone was worried about their loved ones going to war. My sons were in high school and I was glad they didn't have to go to war. I remember the air raid sirens blowing at night and having to turn off our lights. We had black window shades on the windows, so we could draw them and turn the lights back on.

My brother Camillo enlisted in the United States Army and was stationed at Fort Dix, N.J. His basic training was in Camp Croft, South Carolina where he went to school and learned to read and write English. I do not recall what he did while in the service, but I know he did not have to be in the front lines. Camillo brought me a pillow, which I still have when he was honorably discharged from the service. We were happy to have him home and he was anxious to return to work at the Endicott Johnson Shoe Factory.

Leona was eighteen when she went to work in the factory for Endicott Johnson Corporation. Leona gave her entire pay to her father to help support the family. He kept all the money except one dollar, which he gave her. Later she kept the majority of the pay and he kept a small portion. The Remington Rand Corporation started production of airplane parts for the war effort and Leona quit working at Endicott Johnson and went to work for Remington Rand in the Lab.

Joe was 18 years old when he enlisted in the US Army Air force, January 1944. I was not happy but Joe wanted to go in the service. Joe was a sergeant stationed in the South Pacific at the Tinian, Marianas Islands. He was a side blister gunner on a B-29 airplane. While he was stationed in the South Pacific I had a dream about him that his airplane was shot down. In my dream I asked Joe how many men died in the airplane crash. He told me that the pilot and two other men. I was worried and I was going crazy with concern for him. My daughter Leona wrote to our friend Roland Caiozzo, who was in the service stationed around the same area as Joe was. She asked him if he had heard anything about my son Joe. Roland wrote back and said yes. The plane had crashed and he didn't know if Joe was alive, or dead. Joe's airplane crashed on May 7, 1945. We received a letter from Joe telling us what had happened and then we received a letter from the government informing us of the crash.

This is what he wrote, "It took place on my last mission (seventh). We were going on a mission to Oito located on the Japanese island of Kyushu. When we reached the target we ran into some heavy fighter opposition and found ourselves outnumbered seven to one. After we had left the target, we were left with two engines shot out and a third damaged. Our damage was bad enough for us to have to feather the third engine and make a crash landing in the water.

We were less than 100 miles from the coast of Japan when we hit the water. I was thrown clear of the plane after we hit. I found myself under water so I inflated my life preserver, which brought me to the surface. I got to one of the rafts we had gotten out of the plane and joined the rest of the crew. We were in the water a little less than two hours when we sighted a submarine which picked us up.

On the sub they fixed us all up . . . some of the fellows had been wounded over the target and some of us had been injured in the crash. I got out with a cut on my ankle and a few other scratches. Most of us got off pretty lucky. We were on the sub U.S.S. Ray for three days and were then transferred to another sub the U.S.S. Lion Fish to be taken back to our island. In all we spent nine days on the subs. I was up and around the sub on the second day so you see I am O.K."

I was grateful to receive this letter from my son. I had been frantic with worry and I had been praying that he was all right.

We were still at war and I had another dream . . . This was my dream. In the sky there were bunches of clouds. . . on each bunch of clouds there was a table with two people sitting on each cloud, one on either side of the table. I was standing and there were people standing with me.

I asked them, "Do you see what I see?"

My eyes were drawn down to the ground where I saw people sitting in a large circle which was open on one end. The people in the circle were talking and I saw an Angel, he didn't have any wings and he was dressed in white. He was prostrate and he was floating over the top of the circle of people on the ground. His hands were held together like he was praying as he passed over them.

I looked at the circle of people and I saw to one side of the circle a man watching the people. He was dressed in a white robe and had a yellow cord tied around his waist. His hair was long and it fell to his shoulder. I knew that this was Jesus. I woke up . . . I was so frightened, that I was sick for one week.

Rev. Oscar Vitale, Annina and her husband Tony Lauricella were outside of our house talking. I was feeling better and I went outside the house to tell them about my dream.

"In one month the war will be over," I said.

They smiled and said that is impossible. They didn't believe me. In one month there was the end of the war in the Pacific. My dream had come true. I had been right in my interpretation of my dream.

When Gen. Douglas MacArthur, the Supreme Allied Commander, was signing the formal surrender ending the war, which took place on September 2, 1945, my son Joe was in one of the airplanes flying over the ship, USS Missouri. Joe was honorably discharged from the Army Air Force. We were so happy to see him when he came home. He looked like an Angel getting off the train. We went to him and hugged and kissed him. Our family and friends were waiting for us to celebrate and welcome him home. Everybody was hugging and kissing him.

PAOLA'S REMEMBRANCES

My son Melchiore was also in the US Army. He was in the military police. Mitch enlisted in the service in 1945. He told us what happened to him while in the service. This is one of the stories he told us.

"It was 1946, I was with the military police company the 60th military A.S.U. in Mannheim, Germany. We were conducting a police action checking homes for any unauthorized personnel. I was at my post and observed something in the window of a house that did not seem right to me. I told my superior what I observed and my suspicions. We entered the building with weapons drawn and noticed three men and three women. The men were in US uniforms and the women had armbands on with the United States flag on them. They were posing as Americans. We asked the men for identification. They did not have any ID, so we interrogated them. We found out that one of them was a lieutenant in the SS troopers and the other was a Sergeant in the SS troopers. The third man, we called him Scaro, (I do not recall his real name) was Mussolini's bodyguard. He had a large scar across his cheek. We were ready to transport them to the military police station and I noticed that I had forgotten to load my pistol. We left them in the custody of a Lieutenant of the 504th military police and returned to our post.

In 1951 I was in Camp Gordon, Georgia. I met the Lieutenant of the 504th Military police that relieved us when we had left Mannheim. I told him the story of what had happened and asked if he had remembered the incident. He said yes. He told me that Scaro, Mussolini bodyguard made a statement to him.

"If that military policeman (which was me) had turned his head a fraction of an inch I would have killed him."

I proceeded then to tell the Lieutenant that my pistol had not been loaded when we were making the arrest.

He said, "OH MY GOD!"

Mitch re-enlisted in 1949 and became a military police investigator. He picked up AWOL deserters and any other incidents occurring, solving burglary, and crimes for the New York City Police Department, if it had military and civilian personnel involved. He solved some crimes for the FBI. He told us that his commanding officer was shutting down his department for a while. The military prisons were too full and they did not have any more room for the prisoners.

Mitch took a 30 day leave and came home. The commanding officer told Mitch "YOU" are the one who filled all the stockades up, so take it easy till you come back.

Being at war with Italy we couldn't send anything to Sicily. When we were able to get mail through to them I'd enclose an envelope of dried Lipton soup mix in the letters we'd send to them. I also sent them a few dollars to help them buy food. My mother would say to her grandchildren and children, "The bombs will not fall down on us, my grandson is in the airplane and he will not bomb us." My sister told me that she had given her food to the grandchildren and she would go hungry. My

PAOLA'S REMEMBRANCES

dear Mother had a hard life. After the war ended I received a letter from my sister Anna that my mother had died February 1946. She was 82 years old.

My brother Camillo met Rose Catalano and they fell in love. Rose was a warm and generous person. They were married and had a son Michael. We spent many an enjoyable Sunday afternoon at their home. Michael is now married and lives in Florida. Camillo and Rose are no longer with us and we miss them.

My half brother Salvatore (Sam) sent for our niece Mary Napoli Ciaravino, who lived in Castellammare. He asked me if Mary and her children could live with my family when they came to America. I agreed and they came and lived with us for three months. It was hard having so many people living together in our small house. Mary and her daughter did get jobs working at the Endicott Johnson Shoe factory. She saved her money and sent for her husband and the rest of her children. Mary rented our upstairs apartment. When her husband and children came to the United States they moved into the apartment.

Anna Catanzaro my youngest sister wanted to live in the United States. She wrote to me and asked if we would sponsor her family. I asked my husband if he would agree and he did. They arrived in New York City and Calogero and I went to pick them up and brought them back to Endicott. Annina and Gaspare, her husband and their children Melchiore, Vito and Annie stayed with us for a few months. Annina and Gaspere went to work at the Endicott Johnson Shoe Factory. They rented one of the upstairs apartments of our house until they got on their feet and then they bought a house on Arthur Avenue. Annina now lives alone as her husband is gone and her children are grown and on their own. She calls me often on the telephone.

PAOLA'S REMEMBRANCES

**Rosina, Mama, Anna, Francesca, Camillo,
Girolamo, Salvatore, Paola, Agata,
Luminato, Marco, Brigita and Vincenza**

CHAPTER SEVENTEEN

Around 1947 or 1948, my husband decided to open a variety store, Uptown Stationery and Confectionery located on Witherill Street next to the George W. Johnson Elementary School. Leona ran the store for us while my husband continued to work in the Endicott Johnson Shoe factory. It was a small store and business was good. We had a station post office where people could buy stamps and mail their packages. My husband decided to move the store to Oak Hill Avenue. We were at the new location for about two years when my husband decided to dissolve the business.

Leona went to work as a secretary for the Endicott Insurance Agency in 1953 to 1968. Leona loved to sing and has a beautiful mezzo-soprano voice. She joined the Tri Cities Opera Workshop in 1950 and was one of the lead singers in many operatic performances of the Tri Cities Opera productions. She also sang solos in the Bonner Memorial Church choir. Leona met William Davison while he was working for Standard Accident Insurance Company in Canandaigua, New York. Lee and Bill were married July 6, 1968 and moved to Rochester, New York where Bill was employed by the Greece school system as an Instrumental Music Teacher. Later they moved to Buffalo, New York where Bill continued teaching.

Lee and Bill are now retired and live in Apalachin, New York.

My son Joe went to New York State Institute of Applied Arts & Sciences after he returned from the service. He used his G.I. Bill and graduated with an Associate Degree in Chemical Technology. The college is now called Broome Community College. Joe moved to Schenectady and went to work for General Electric in Schenectady, New York where he met Jane Kinns and her three year old son David Pashley. Joe and Jane were married and now live in Scotia, New York. They have three beautiful children, Joel, and twin sons Matthew, and Mark. David married Marian Bisner and they have two lovely children Danny and Melanie. David works for the Freihofer Company. Joel their oldest son went to the University of Rochester, New York and at Penn State for his master's degree in geology. Joel is married to Jean McGuire and they live in Ringe, New Hampshire, Joel works in Lincoln, Massachusetts. Matt and Mark also went to the University of Buffalo and at Rochester Institute of Technology. They live in Scotia, New York and work as steel detailers for Upstate Detailing, in Burnt Hills, New York.

Joe is now enjoying his retirement from General Electric. I talk to him on the phone and he comes to see me when he can.

My son Melchiore (Mitch) was discharged from the Army in 1953. When he came home he went to work at Endicott Johnson for one week and then he went to work for the Ozalid Company in the film-shipping department. He worked thirty two and a half years for Ozalid. Mitch had a lot of girl friends and I recall one particular girl. I don't remember her name but I didn't like her. She came to Endicott with her girl friend to visit my son and they stayed overnight in our home. I did not like the way they were acting and I told them to leave.

"Mitch, I do not want these girls in my house another minute. Take them home," I said.

Mitch saw how upset I was and told the girls to get ready as he was going to drive them home.

Finally Mitch met the right girl, Sylvia DeBloom and they fell in love. Mitch and Sylvia were married in the Fairview Methodist Church in Binghamton, NY. They have three children, a daughter Michele and two sons, John and Michael. Michele was around one year old when Sylvia went back to work. She asked me if I would take care of her baby. I recall one snowy day when Mitch was bringing Michele over to our house and I was looking out the back kitchen window that faces the patio when I saw Mitch walking on the patio with Michele in his arms. The patio had ice and snow on it and Mitch fell on his back with Michele in his arms. I ran out the back door and tried to help him up.

"No Ma, take the baby. I'm all right," said Mitch.

I took Michele from him and brought her into the house. It was a joy and a privilege taking care of Michele. I enjoyed having her around the house.

Michele now lives in Susquehanna, Pennsylvania with her daughter Robyn, and she works in Montrose Pennsylvania, at the Endless

PAOLA'S REMEMBRANCES

Mountain Hospital, as an assistant supervisor in the laboratory. John works in Ithaca, New York as a senior police sergeant and in Dryden, New York as a detective. John and his wife Teri have two sons, Justin and Jarron. Michael is a graduate of Ithaca College.

My daughter Annie at the age of 16 went to work in the fine welt annex factory, of the Endicott Johnson Shoe Company. Annie brought home her paycheck to my husband. He kept the entire check, and gave her 50 cents back. If she needed something he would give her money to buy it. The money was used to pay the mortgage on the house.

Annie was 18 years old when she met Edward Popelka. Eddie worked for Endicott Johnson in the same factory Annie did. He would come over to her work area and talk to her. Eddie wanted to take Annie out, but Annie told him that he would have to talk to her father first. Eddie was very nervous having to ask my husband's permission to date Annie. He knew he would have to do this if they were going to date, so he went to the store where my husband was working. Eddie was standing at the front counter and he picked up something off the counter top, I do not know what it was and it fell out of his hand breaking the show case glass. Eddie was mortified and offered to pay for the broken glass. My husband realized Eddie was embarrassed and he felt bad for him. Eddie paid for the broken glass and Calogero was very impressed with Eddie. He gave his permission for Annie and Eddie to start their courtship but there were rules they had to follow. They could go out

Francesca Paolina Curatolo

only on Saturday night, but they had to be home by 10:00 p.m. Annie and Eddie started to date and they obeyed his rules. When they came home they would stand on the back porch and talk.

We had an engagement party for Annie and Eddie and they were married May 30, 1953. They have one adopted son, James Edward. James married Lois Gleason and he is very happy working in Wilson Memorial Hospital's laboratory.

Eddie is no longer with us. He passed away August 1976. He was a kind person and it was a great loss for all of us. He was loved and respected by all of my family and we miss him very much. Annie and Eddie were married for twenty three years. Annie lives alone in their home at Glendale Drive.

Fran graduated from the Union Endicott high school in 1953. She went to work at the George F. Johnson Memorial Library in Endicott. Agatha graduated from the Union Endicott high school in 1954.

I have been very happy living in Endicott with my husband and children and remembering the good times we had together. I recall the spaghetti suppers we gave at the Bonner Memorial Presbyterian Church. My husband and I along with Mr. & Mrs. Patsy Muggeo, Mrs. Calogera Fantuzzo, Mrs. Liodici, Mrs. Elodia Tedeschi, Mrs. Fanelli, Mrs. Sotis and Anna and Tony Lauricella to name a few helped with the preparation of the food. The ladies aid society sponsored the church supper. We had a wonderful time in fellowship with the members of our church and our friends.

PAOLA'S REMEMBRANCES

I became a Deacon of the Bonner Memorial Presbyterian Church. One of my duties was to prepare the communion bread and fill the wine glasses for Communion Sunday. I ironed the Communion tablecloth along with my other duties. My husband also was a Deacon of the church.

Francesca Paolina Curatolo

**Bonner Memorial Presbyterian Church
and
Our home on North McKinley Avenue**

PAOLA'S REMEMBRANCES

Calogero in front of our store

Francesca Paolina Curatolo

Our 25th Wedding Anniversary (1947)

CHAPTER EIGHTEEN

It was 1955, when my husband and I decided to build a new house. We bought a lot on the corner of Smith and Wilson Avenue in Endwell, New York.

Calogero hired a contractor Gulio, to build the new house. Calogero and my son Melchiore, along with Tony Ciaravino and Gaspare Catanzaro, helped with building the house. It is a beautiful brick ranch style home. The living room was large and it has a fireplace three bedrooms, a bath, kitchen and a den. In the basement we had a beauty shop for my daughter Francie. On the west side of the house was a driveway that led into a garage. The back yard had a garden and beautiful flowers were growing around the house. We had many a party on the patio. My daughters Leona, Fran and Agatha lived with us in this house. I loved this house that my husband built for me.

It was on a Sunday evening when Calogero started to have chest pains and his shoulders hurt. My son Mitch was trying to help him by massaging his back and shoulders. We called Doctor Maggiore and he came to the house on McKinley Avenue. The Doctor came in and examined Calogero. He told us Calogero was having a heart attack and to call the ambulance and take him to the hospital. Calogero was in the hospital for about two weeks. During the next thirteen years he had about six heart attacks and was unable to work and had to retire. He had worked for Endicott Johnson 35 years.

In 1960 my daughters Agatha and Francie decided to move to California. They didn't tell my husband what they were planning. They thought that once they were in Los Angeles, he would agree and let them stay. He did not and was very upset. He'd walk up and down the sidewalk in front of the house crying. Leona wrote to Aggie and Fran and she told them that their father was distraught, and wanted them to come home. They did come home to please him and he was happy again. Fran didn't want to return to her job at the Library so she went to beauty school and became a hairdresser. Agatha went back to work for Metropolitan Insurance Company.

Calogero was 70 years old when he passed away on February 6, 1968. I felt lost and empty without him. I miss him very much.

PAOLA'S REMEMBRANCES
CHAPTER NINETEEN

March, 1969 my daughters Agatha, Fran and I decided to move to California. My husband's sister Anna was living in San Fernando Valley.

We stayed with her for a month and than we rented an apartment in North Hollywood. Agatha went to work for Metropolitan Life Insurance Company in Hollywood and Fran worked in Los Angeles for Shareholders Mutual Fund Company in the International Division. She was laid off because the International Division was moving to England. Aggie told Fran to put her application in at Metropolitan Life Insurance Company and she did. Fran started working for Metropolitan in the Hollywood Branch and later in Encino and Canoga Park Metropolitan offices.

I loved living in California because the weather reminded me of the weather in Castellammare. We became close to my sister-in-law Anna and her husband Tony. We spent many happy times with them, along with our friend John Caiozzo, Joe, Henriette and Claudette Musa and their families.

My youngest daughter Agatha met Ronald Burks while we were living in North Hollywood and they started dating. Ron was born in Modesto, California and he has a daughter Mary from a previous marriage. Mary lives in Michigan and has two son's David and Matthew, two granddaughters and two grandsons. Agatha and Ron were married

February 14, 1970. Ron is wonderful man whenever we need any help he is always there for us. They have two children Charles and Lydiann. Aggie decided to return to work at Metropolitan Life Insurance Company after the birth of Charlie and she asked me if I would take care of him. When Aggie came home from work to pick him up, Charlie wanted to stay with me and not go home with her. Charlie is very close to me and I know he loves me. We have a very special bond. He calls me almost everyday to see how I am and if I need anything. I love him very much.

It was 1973, Aggie had just given birth to Lydiann when Ron was laid off from Lockheed. There was a recession and he was having difficulty finding work in Los Angeles, so he asked us if we would like to move back to Endicott with them and we said yes. Fran just had an operation and she was at a point in her life that she was ready for a change. We called my family in Endicott and told them we had decided to move back to Endicott and they were very happy. My son Mitch said he would check to see if there were any openings for Ron in the factory where he was working. Aggie and Fran were working for Metropolitan in the Canoga Park office. They asked for a transfer to the Binghamton Metropolitan Office, but Fran was the only one who was transferred, Aggie had to resign. We made plans to sell some of our furniture and the rest we had a moving truck bring to Annie and Eddie's house where we were going to stay until we could find an apartment. Fran and I flew from the Los Angeles Airport to the Broome County Airport and

Ron and Aggie and the children drove back to Endicott. We had been in Endicott for a week or so when Ron and Aggie and the children arrived. My daughter Lee came from Buffalo to see me and take me back to Buffalo with them for a visit. I stayed with Lee for a month and then I returned to Endicott where we rented an apartment on Camelot Road in Endwell.

One day Fran came home and told Aggie that Metropolitan was looking for an office clerk. Aggie applied for the position and she started working that next week. She was happy to have gotten the job so quickly. Ron was hired by GAF and he started working a split shift. He'd take care of the children when he was home and I took care of Charlie and Lydiann when they were working.

I was happy to be back in Endicott with all my children, but I missed California and its beautiful warm weather. It felt strange being back in Endicott and seeing how much it had changed in the past five years. Endicott had a saying ... Which way E. J. This was the land of the Square Deal where my husband had worked for over thirty years in the Endicott Johnson Shoe factory and where we brought up our children. The Endicott Johnson tannery factory on Oak Hill Avenue was no longer in operation and they had torn down all the factories. IBM was growing and they had purchased all of the former lands of E.J. and began replacing them with new plants and buildings. I felt sad seeing the changes in E.J. What happened to the company that was owned by George F. Johnson. We respected George F., a generous man who believed that if you paid your employees a good wage they would lead normal happy lives. He built homes for his employees and gave them the opportunity to purchase these homes at cost, which was $2,500 to $3,500 depending on what model home you bought. We had bought our home so we didn't take this offer, but those who were interested in buying a home paid for them by having the mortgage payment deducted from their pay checks each week. If you couldn't make the payment that week all you had to do is to contact the payroll office and they would not take it out that week. George F. gave much to his employees. When we were in need and there were times we were, my husband would ask E.J. for help. One of the things they gave us was a load of coal for heating our home.

It was in 1978 when Fran decided to buy a house on Nebraska Avenue in Endwell New York. We were happy living in this home. I kept myself busy crocheting afghans, doilies, slippers, baby sweaters, and hats and sold them at craft shows.

PAOLA'S REMEMBRANCES

**Paola Russo Curatolo
May 10, 1980
76 Years Old**

Francesca Paolina Curatolo

Fran and my grandson Charlie opened a computer and video store in 1989. Charlie worked during the day and Fran worked evenings after she was through working at the library. They had a good business at first, but after a year they decided to close the store due to the big video stores moving into town and they couldn't compete with them. That was about the time that I started not feeling well. I was having mini strokes. Fran and I lived fourteen years in this house and then we moved to an apartment on Andrews Avenue in Endicott and later to the Glenpark Mews apartments.

Agatha works for Columbian Mutual Insurance Company and is planning her retirement. Ron worked for Anitec for 25 years, but the plant closed and he will retire in a few years also. Lydiann married Michael Farruggio and they have two beautiful children, Andrea and Alicia. Charlie married Deborah Wyatt and they have two handsome boys, Charles Ronald Benjamin Burks Jr., and Christopher Mark Burks.

Fran worked for Metropolitan until 1980 when they put her on part time, so she applied for another part time job at the George F. Johnson Library and was working two places. A full time position became available in the library as senior library clerk. She accepted the position supervising the clerical staff and resigned from Metropolitan.

As the years went by I started to have problems with my heart. Leona would take care of me during the day and Fran took care of me at night. Fran retired from the library November, 1997 and she takes care of me now.

I have seen many changes since my return to Endicott. E. J. was sold and the one plant left on Glendale Drive in Endicott closed their doors this year. IBM started to streamline their operations offering early retirement to their employee's downsizing their work force and making many changes. Endicott is no longer the industrial community it once was. The era for a small businessman is gone, but I hope and pray that one day it will be as it once was.

Francesca Paolina Curatolo

**My children celebrating my 94th Birthday
Agatha, Paola, Joseph, Anna, Francesca, Melchiore,
Leona**

PAOLA'S REMEMBRANCES

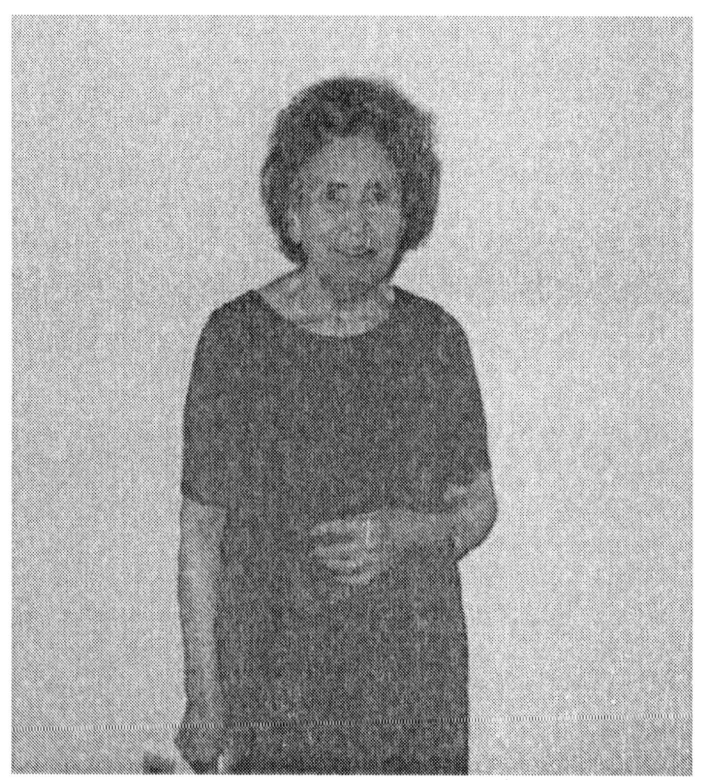

My 95th Birthday

Francesca Paolina Curatolo

My Dream About Mama

Throughout my life I have dreams in which I was searching for my mother. All the times that I have dreamt about her I could not find her in my dreams. After more than ninety three years I had a dream. This was the first time I saw my mother. She was standing alone in a field. It didn't have any grass on it just dirt.

I was about 20 feet away from her. I saw her dressed in a long white gown with long sleeves and around her waist she had a small yellow ribbon tied around it falling down to her right side. She looked so beautiful. Her hair was white and looked just like a white cloud and there was light radiating through it. It shone like sunlight. Her hair was full, not how she wore it when she was young. She was standing and I heard a voice. I don't know where the voice came from and I didn't see anyone else. It was a man's voice. The voice spoke in English it came from a distance.

The voice said, "You won."

My mother didn't say anything and didn't move, she just stood there. I went closer to her.

I asked her, "What did you win?"

She didn't say anything. I woke up and I was happy to have dreamt this beautiful dream.

I said, "God Blessed my Mother."

I know now she is with God and was happy to see my mother that way. I never saw my mother dressed this way when she was alive. My mother's face was young and it was aglow. I knew it was her by her presence but I didn't see the features of her face when I went to her and stood by her side. I have not dreamt about her since this dream.

I am ninety five years old, I have had a full life, and I hope to live to be 100 years old. I am proud of all my children and grandchildren they are beautiful and I love them each and everyone very much. My wish for my children and my grandchildren is health and happiness. I pray to God to give *la salvezza del la anima, la pace e la salute,* the salvation of their souls, peace and health. May God recompense all the good things that have been done for me and give double back to my children and grandchildren. *Dio ti benedici,* God bless you.

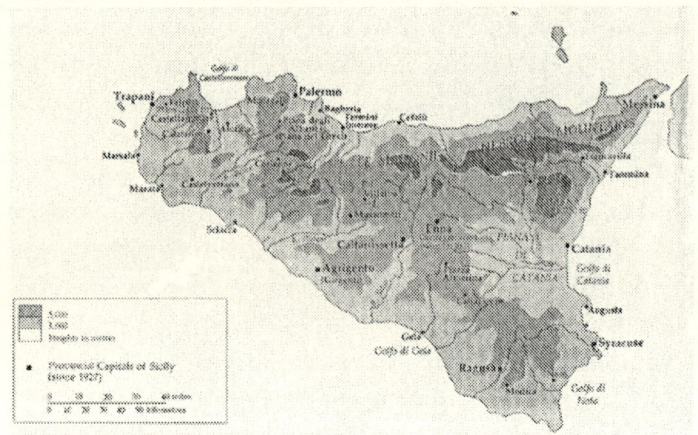

SICILY

Sicily is the largest island in the Mediterranean Sea, (9,926 square miles in area, pop. 4,863,587) almost the size of Belgium. The Strait of Messina separates Sicily from the mainland of Italy.

In ancient times it was called Trinacria, because of its triangular shape represented symbolically by three human legs bent as if running, extended from a Gorgon's head adorned with intertwined snakes. This representation gave Sicily its coat of arms.

For four thousand years' travelers and conquerors differing in nationality, race and religion have been drawn to Sicily. Discoveries of cave drawings and tools show that prehistoric people lived in what is now Sicily.

The following were invaders: The Sikelian, Carthaginians, Greeks and Romans. The Germanic invasion of Vandals and Ostrogoths. The Byzantine

Empire, North African Muslims. The Saracens, Arabs. The Norman's, the Germans and French, Spain, Savoy and Austria. The Italian patriot Giuseppe Garibaldi invaded Sicily in May 11, 1860 and finally the Allies during World War II invaded Sicily on July 10, 1943.

Francesca Paolina Curatolo

Epilogue

On November 30, 1998 Paola Russo Curatolo went to be with her Lord and Savior Jesus Christ. Mama, God saw you were getting tired, so He put his arms around you and whispered, "Come to Me." Not a day passes that we don't think of you, love you and feel the loss of you. While you have physically left us, your spirit surrounds us and we continue to feel your love and your warmth. You will be sorely missed and you are held dearly in our hearts and memories.

Mama, we lived together for sixty four years and I give thanks for having you as my mother, friend and companion. You were a strong person, open minded and understanding. Your love for your family was unwavering. There were many times we would have long talks and you would give me your advice and guidance. It has been very hard not having you in the house with me, but I still talk to you and you are with me in spirit. I miss you very much. I love you Mama... Francie.

I remember when Mama would pack a little lunch on a nice summer day and take us for a long walk. We'd go as far as Hayes Avenue from North McKinley Avenue. Joe, Menzie, Annie and I would be excited because we were going to pick berries in the woods. We'd get hungry so we would have our snack and we ate most of the berries we picked. This was fun... Lee

PAOLA'S REMEMBRANCES

Mama I miss hearing your words "Joe your here" whenever I came home to see you. I remember the times you fought off the neighbor bully to protect me. I remember your caring for me when I was a frail and sickly youth. I was always grateful for the care and worry while I was away in the Air Force. Most of all I'm grateful that you were my Mama... Joe

I was born on July 23, 1927 and Mama you held me and loved me. I remember the first time I was in the crib and you were mopping the floor in the kitchen. You made sure you fed us all first and then you fixed your own meal. You made our clothes because Pa was the only one working. You brought up six children, I don't know how you did it, but we all turned out okay. You will always be in my heart. I know I gave you a hard time as I was growing up, but you were always there when I needed you. When I went into the Army in 1945, I was camping out with the other solders and it was cold and raining. I was so cold the first words that came out of my mouth were "Ma I'm Cold." You always made me feel safe and warm. You were there to comfort me when I was born and I was there to comfort you when you died. I didn't want you to leave me. I miss you and you will always be in my heart. Thank you for being my Mama... Mitch

Mama, coming to see you each week these past years for me were happy moments and are precious to me. We would sit at the dinning room table talking and reminiscing. One of the things I remember as a child is coming home from school and you were in the kitchen and the smell of freshly baked bread filling the room. You had on your apron and around your head was a towel. On the table was freshly baked bread made into Easter baskets that had a hard boiled egg in them. Mama you are special and I thank you for all you did for us all. . . Annie

The pain is still great, but the memories help to fill the void in our hearts. God blessed us with a caring, loving Mother and Grandmother. We will always be grateful to him. Mama you will never be forgotten. You will always be in our thoughts and prayers. We will do our best to make you proud. We love and miss you. . . Aggie.

As a young child, you cared for me while my parents Mitch and Sylvia worked. You let me play as I pleased, often taking the pots and pans out of the cupboard, putting them all over the floor and never said "No." The holidays, especially Christmas with our family's Sicilian traditional of Calamari, smelt, octopus, tripe and your wonderful cannoli, pizzelles and homemade pasta showed what a wonderful cook you were. For Christmas, when I was 13 years old you crocheted a tablecloth for my hope chest. Through the years you gave me doilies you had crocheted. When I was young you sewed clothes for me. Your handwork was beautiful. After Grandpa passed away you, Aunt Fran and Aunt Aggie went to live in California. I missed all of you, but I especially missed you. I felt as though I had lost you forever. When you would come back to visit I would not want to leave your side. It would make you feel bad when I would cry at the thought of your visit coming to an end, but you knew how much I loved you. The love you had for us was unconditional and without judgment. Your ability to accept life's challenges put you ahead of your time. The love I have for you is a deep and powerful feeling. I was blessed to have you in my life for forty years and to have my daughter Robyn know and love you. Your loving and caring influence in my life will always be with me. I hope that when grandchildren are a part of my life I can give to them the ways you have given to me and your unconditional love. Thank you for the memories... Michele

To my beloved Aunt Paola who was there for me when the Lord took my precious mother Agata. Aunt Paola will always be in my prayers and my heart, for I love her as much as if she was like my own mother. . . Rosie Gance Poss.

My Aunt Pauline's mark in my life can be summed up in this scripture, "Blessed are the pure in heart for they shall see God." (Matt5:8) It was simple to understand my Aunt's love for the Lord, as her pure heart lent a hand in pointing the way to Him for any who touched her life, including mine. . . Claudia Gance Wescott.

I remember when it was Great Grandma's birthday and Aunt Fran was giving her a birthday party. I was 5 years old and came in the house to see Grandma and I wished her happy birthday. I gave her a birthday card and she hugged and kissed me. She was happy to see me. Great Grandma was always good to me. She made me Farina whenever I came to see her and I loved it. I lived next door to her and visited her every day. When I had to leave and go home she'd say to me, I love you Andrea. The last time I saw Grandma was in the hospital. She was in bed and her eyes were closed, and I had to leave her and go home. I said goodbye to her and I told her I loved her. I am 7 years old now and I still remember Great Grandma. I love you Great Grandma and I miss you very much...Andrea Paola Farruggio

Grandma, It's taken me along time to write this, as I still have not come to terms with your death. I always thought that you'd be immortal. I found out that your body wasn't immortal, but your spirit is. Not a day goes by that I don't think of you, or what you did for me all these years. I know at times I disappointed you, but you never let it show. When I still call the house I half expect to hear, Char is that you, and as always I told you I loved you. I can't bring myself to think that your gone, even if deep down I know that your strengths and beliefs brought you somewhere there was no pain and that you were back with your husband. Well now through tears I say my last goodbye; Goodbye to your body on earth, but not that you're ever far from my heart or soul. As you watch over me from where ever that beautiful place may be. I'll do my best to make you proud to say, "Yes that's my grandson" in loving memory... "Your Char"
7-4-2001

Family Lineage

I am Paola Russo. I was born on November 9, 1903, in Castellammare Del Golfo, which is in the Provincia of Trapani, Sicily, to Melchiore Russo and Anna Ganci.

Paola Tamburella Ganci and Francesco Ganci were my mother's parents; Brigita and Luminato Russo was my father's.

My father had three wives. Vincenza, (I do not know her maiden name), was his first wife, they had three sons and a daughter: Luminato, Marco, Girolamo and Brigita. Vincenza was taken ill and died.

Agata Randazzo, his second wife was a widow. She brought with her a son, Giuseppe Randazzo. Agata and Papa had two children: a daughter Vincenza and a son Salvatore. Agata died when the children were young.

His third marriage was to Anna Ganci, my mother. They had six children, a son Camillo and five daughters Agata, Paola, Rosina, Francesca and Anna.

Papa raised thirteen children. His children from the first two marriages were grown and out on their own when he married my mother.

Girolamo joined the Italian Naval Service and when he was discharged, he sailed to the United States and settled in Detroit, Michigan. Luminato

Francesca Paolina Curatolo

and Marco were mariners on steamships. Marco and Luminato left the mariners and Marco settled in South Africa, Luminato went to New Orleans, Louisiana. Salvatore, Pa's son from his second marriage, immigrated to Detroit Michigan.

Brigita, Pa's daughter by his first marriage and Vincenza his daughter by his second marriage moved to Argentina. Brigita met Giuseppe Napoli and married him. Vincenza married Giuseppe's brother Marco. Brigita and Giuseppe made their home in Argentina. Vincenza and Marco lived in Argentina for short time and then returned to Castellammare with their children.

PAOLA'S REMEMBRANCES

FAMILY TREE

Calogero Curatolo
Born: 24 September 1898
Castellammare Del Golfo, Sicily

Died: 6 February 1968
Father: Guiseppe Curatolo
Mother: Leonarda Messina Curatolo

Paola Russo
Born: 9 November 1903
Castellammare Del Golfo, Sicily
Died: 30 November 1998
Father: Melchiore Russo
Mother: Anna Ganci Russo

Married 16 December 1922

———————— 4 Daughters 2 Sons ————————
↓

Daughter -Leona C. Curatolo
M: William Davison No Children

Son - Joseph C. Curatolo
M: Jane Kinns

↓	↓	↓
Children:	**Children:**	**Children:**
Joel Curatolo	Matthew Curatolo	Mark Curatolo
M: Jean McGuire	No Children	No Children

Francesca Paolina Curatolo

Son - Melchiore Curatolo
M: Sylvia DeBloom

↓	↓	↓
Children: Michele Curatolo	**Children:** John Curatolo M:Terri Briggs	**Children:** Michael Curatolo No Children
↓	↓	↓
Children: Robyn White	**Children:** Justin Curatolo	**Children:** Jarron Curatolo

Daughter - Anna Curatolo
M: Edward J. Popelka

↓

Children:
James E. Popelka
M: Lois Gleason

Daughter - Francesca P. Curatolo
No Children

Daughter - Agatha R.L. Curatolo
M: Ronald F. Burks

↓	↓
Children: Lydiann F. Burks M: Michael Farruggio	**Children:** Charles W. A. Burks M: Deborah Wyatt

↓	↓	↓	↓
Children: Andrea P. Farruggio	**Children:** Alicia T. Farruggio	**Children:** Charles R.B. Burks Jr.	**Children:** Christopher M. Burks

PAOLA'S REMEMBRANCES

About the Author

Francesca Paolina Curatolo was born in Endicott, New York a small Village in Upstate New York. She is a graduate of the Union Endicott High School and the Imperial School of Beauty. Ms. Curatolo is retired and lives with her little dog Precious, a Bichion Frise. Although she is retired she likes to keep busy by working as a substitute for the Union-Endicott Central School District. She enjoys making crafts with her Grand nieces and nephews, cooking, reading, music, gardening and crocheting.

Printed in the United States
1052100004B